History without Chronology

Stefan Tanaka

LEVER PRESS

Lever Press (leverpress.org) is a publisher of pathbreaking scholarship. Supported by a consortium of liberal arts institutions focused on, and renowned for, excellence in both research and teaching, our press is grounded on three essential commitments: to be a digitally native press, to be a peer-reviewed, open access press that charges no fees to either authors or their institutions, and to be a press aligned with the ethos and mission of liberal arts colleges.

The complete manuscript of this work was subjected to a partly closed ("single blind") review process. For more information, please see our Peer Review Commitments and Guidelines at https://www.leverpress.org/peerreview

DOI: https://doi.org/10.3998/mpub.11418981
Print ISBN: 978-1-64315-003-1
Open access ISBN: 978-1-64315-004-8

Library of Congress Control Number: 2019938043

Published in the United States of America by Lever Press, in partnership with Amherst College Press and Michigan Publishing

Contents

Acknowledgments

Recently, I have been reminded that I have been working on pasts and history and time for decades. It makes me wonder to what extent my thinking has changed over the past thirty years! I think it has; yet such reminders point to repetition and hopes for improvement. But above all, it suggests that I have received the help of a large number of friends, colleagues, and institutions. These acknowledgments will no doubt overlook many— my apologies.

In a sense, this manuscript has three origins. First, my recognition that time is an abstraction, not only something learned but something social and historical, came at an everyday moment. My then young daughter, who has a diurnal clock, came into our room on a weekend, asking if we were getting up. "Not until seven o'clock" was the answer. She returned several times in approximately five minute intervals but then stopped; it was well after seven. It turned out that she became preoccupied and missed the moment when the minute hand reached twelve. She was waiting, now very patiently, for *precisely* seven o'clock. I learned something important that day; this turned my attention to not just pasts and history but time as an abstract concept, its connection to history, and how it orders our lives.

I did not realize what I was getting into; it has been an intellectually enjoyable and stimulating yet long and meandering sojourn. Like so many historians, I figured I knew something about time. After teaching several seminars on time and space (once with Jim Fujii), I realized that I needed to concentrate on time. Back then, I believed that historians had not written much on time; perhaps that is true, but I now realize that there is a considerable literature on time throughout the recorded past. I am continuing to read, learn, and change my way of thinking. Many people and institutions have aided me as I wander through the thicket of writings. In particular, I have been guided by mentors and friends: Harry Harootunian, Luce Giard, and the late Masao Miyoshi. Harry continues to inspire, Luce in her elegant yet determined way kept me focused, and Masao showed me that I could move beyond my training in the history of modern Japan (and cajoled me forward). Each person set a tenor of inquiry, a high standard that started with my mentors Harry and Tetsuo Najita.

Meetings, such as the symposium on "four modernities" at Witswaterand University organized by Dilip Menon, gave me confidence to see my work beyond Japan to Asia; the conferences of the International Network on Theory in History helped me decenter geography from my analyses. Berber Bevernage and his colleagues at Ghent have developed a wonderful occasion for ideas in history. And it was at a conference on historiography in Athens where the lecture by Antonis Liakos on modern Greek historiography helped me see the breadth of the system—in my mind, I replaced Greek with Japanese, and the isomorphism of temporal hierarchy in modern history was uncanny.

The second origin occurred in a not-always-scintillating meeting (more than fifteen years ago) where the topic was the "death" of print publishing in the face of the internet. I commented to Michael Grossberg that we should do something to make the internet suitable for historical communication, not wait for it to change how history published. As a forward-looking editor, he responded something like, "Good idea, Stefan; you do something." This began my inquiry into digital media, the digital humanities, and now scholarly communication.

This is the second rabbit hole—the intersection of digital media and academia. On the one hand, I embarked on a typical digital humanities track. I created a project and began to port material to the digital interface. My muse in this adventure has been Jan Reiff, who has provided sage advice as well as well as conversations that this exploration with digital media could be more. My first foray presenting research in the digital humanities was at the Conference on Digital Research in the Humanities and Arts at Dartington. Thank you to Barry Smith and the committee for including me and to Ric Allsopp and Scott Delahunta for including my essay in *Performance Research* (2006). I was reminded that digital media also has a history (cliometrics) at the University of Wisconsin, Milwaukee; thank you to Doug Howland for the opportunity. For some reason, Kenneth Price, Katherine Walter, and William Thomas invited me to the Nebraska Digital Workshop, University of Nebraska, Lincoln, in 2010. This was an important moment, reaffirming what I was trying to do but forcing me to consider time much more seriously than I had. Moreover, this was, and I hope is, a part of the future of the digital humanities, helping us think differently about scholarship, understanding, and dissemination. Finally, I must acknowledge the collegiality and collaboration of Jessica Pressman, Katherine Hijar, and Maura Giles-Watson. Through SD|DH (San Diego Digital Humanities), we worked to foster institutional presence (and to provide moral support/therapy) in the digital humanities locally.

The third moment came amid my waywardness, reading and thinking about time and history but without clear direction. Kwai Ng, my colleague in sociology, called and asked me to present the Joseph Gusfield Lecture and suggested the surreptitious title of the last seminar I taught in the history department, "History as Media." In the course of our discussion, I suggested "History without Chronology." This led to my *Public Culture* essay—I'm thankful to Fred Turner for encouraging me to submit my work to that fine journal. This book is an expanded (and modified) version of the inquiry I broached in that essay.

This book would not have been possible without the environment of the University of California, San Diego (UCSD)—both because and in spite of it. Above all, it is a place where contacts beyond disciplines are possible, though not without contention. First, when I relocated from history to the Department of Communication, I encountered Robert Horwitz; I send thanks to him for getting this going (my discussions started when Robert and I found ourselves in physical therapy sessions following operations). I knew life would be better but had little idea how liberating it would become. This comment is not to be read as a criticism of my previous department; it is a worry on the ways that disciplines discipline, a tendency that often fosters risk-adverse intellectual practices. Academics all know this; I am still learning the different ways it happens. In short, I can now think about history in addition to practicing history. I am deeply grateful to all my colleagues in the department for our intellectually vibrant environment. The Laboratory for Comparative Human Development, founded and directed by Michael Cole, was a terrific environment for thinking about the processes and ideas of development and temporality. I thank Mike and the many people who visited and participated in the lab. Geof Bowker has become an important friend and confidant, which began in a class on time to first-year students that we taught outside of our home departments. I was able to teach a class on cybernetics through the Macy Foundation conferences with Deborah Forster and Eric Leonardis—it was a weekly adventure. An important respite from UCSD was opened up by a visiting position at UCLA for two quarters as the Terasaki chair for US-Japan relations. Thank you, Bill Marotti, for making it possible; thanks as well to our class and the class with Jan on the digital humanities. When I returned to

UCSD and was trying to figure out how to foster activities in Japanese studies after several departures, Seth Lerer convinced me to apply to be director and restart the Center for the Humanities. His action further convinced me that there were many ways to work beyond our silos; ideas matter. The center, with the able partnership of Sarah McCollough, the associate director, helped me transform ideas into programs. In talking to students over the years, I realize the different classes I taught turned out to have a similar theme: time. They perhaps saw it before I did. More important, they persevered. While I hope they learned, those classes certainly helped me work through these ideas. My thanks to Christina Aushana, Michael Berman, Waqas Butt, Orianna Cacchione, Yelena Gluzman, Jacob Hellman, Ramsey Ismail, Jessica Jordan, Ji Hee Jung, Satoko Kakihara, Jack Jin Gary Lee, Kate McDonald, Stephen Mandiberg, Ryan Moran, Jon Paden, Erika Ramirez, Brizila Rodriguez, Tomoyuki Sasaki, Yi Hong Sim, Katie Simpson, Tad Skotnicki, George Solt, Jonathan Walton, and Rika Yonemura. To emphasize that these classes were often conceptually fraught, I paraphrase Gary, who recently told me that the class he took still haunts him. For me, that's high praise!

Several events and people have helped in the writing of this book. It has been quite a test to keep it relatively brief, set the right tone, and convey the gist of the message. The Gusfield lecture got me off to a good start, and attempts to present my work through PechaKucha-style presentations helped me think of concision and audience. The Nebraska Digital Workshop was the most memorable event (for a fun but less-than-successful sprint). Several friends have provided invaluable suggestions on earlier versions of this manuscript; thank you to Michael Berman, Geof Bowker, Michael Cole, Edward Dickinson, Sally Deutsch, Erin Glass, Katherine Hijar, Robert Horwitz, Helge Jordheim, Howard Kushner, Jay Lemke, Chris Lorenz, Jessica Pressman, Hillel Schwartz, and Espen Ytreberg. Of course, I thank the anonymous reviewers for their generous and constructive reading.

This work benefited from important institutional support. First, I was able to read and write a draft during a yearlong sabbatical from UCSD. The academic senate of UCSD has generously provided research grants at different points of my inquiry, but there is another part of the senate that has directly, and intellectually, contributed to this work. We frequently see university and professional service as taking away from research. The meetings are often boring, yet I have had many fruitful conversations with colleagues on academic senate committees. Those discussions show up in this book; in particular, I have fond memories of conversations about time with Henry Abarbanel, Farrell Ackerman, and Katja Lindenberg. Finally, I recently returned from a stimulating and generative few months at the Center for Advanced Study at the Norwegian Academy of Science and Letters as a research fellow of the project "Insync: How Synchronization and Mediation Produce Collective Times, Then and Now," directed by Helge Jordheim and Espen Ytreberg. It was a home of major, though off-center intellectuals (e.g., three historians, none in a history department) who share a related interest in history, media, and time. I was able to improve, correct, and hone the manuscript as a visiting researcher at the warm and intellectually vital center. Unfortunately, I learned of many topics, issues, and people I should have known about before writing and incorporated into this book. I now have ideas for future research on what histories without chronology might be.

Work in the digital humanities also made me aware of new modes of scholarly communication, including open access. There is much hope for more interactive forms of publishing that use the affordances of digital media. Margy Avery has provided important support and encouragement and, in particular, made me aware of Lever Press, and an exchange with Lisa Trivedi helped me decide. Beth Bouloukos has the unenviable position of building a portfolio for a new press that is looking forward while negotiating the world of inherited practices and institutions. Thank you, Beth, for keeping the hope of new forms of scholarly communication alive.

Also, thank you to Amanda Karby for shepherding this manuscript through the press.

Most important, I thank my family. Kyoko has been wonderfully supportive even on weekends as I labored on this project. The long gestation for this book coincides with the lifetimes of Alisa and Keenan. They have gracefully shared the presence of these ideas and humored—and at times even respected—quips on time and history. This book is dedicated to them, in the hopes that they will continue to honor but not be unnecessarily beholden to the past.

Member Institution Acknowledgments

Lever Press is a joint venture. This work was made possible by the generous support of Lever Press member libraries from the following institutions:

Adrian College
Agnes Scott College
Allegheny College
Amherst College
Bard College
Berea College
Bowdoin College
Carleton College
Claremont Graduate
    University
Claremont McKenna College
Clark Atlanta University
Coe College
College of Saint Benedict /
    Saint John's University
The College of Wooster

Denison University
DePauw University
Earlham College
Furman University
Grinnell College
Hamilton College
Harvey Mudd College
Haverford College
Hollins University
Keck Graduate Institute
Kenyon College
Knox College
Lafayette College Library
Lake Forest College
Macalester College
Middlebury College

Morehouse College
Oberlin College
Pitzer College
Pomona College
Rollins College
Santa Clara University
Scripps College
Sewanee: The University
   of the South
Skidmore College
Smith College
Spelman College
St. Lawrence University

St. Olaf College
Susquehanna University
Swarthmore College
Trinity University
Union College
University of Puget Sound
Ursinus College
Vassar College
Washington and Lee
   University
Whitman College
Willamette University
Williams College

To
Alisa and Keenan

INTRODUCTION

Recast in the mold of a taxonomic ordering of things, chronology becomes the alibi of time, a way of making use of time without reflecting on it.

—Michel de Certeau (1986: 216)

[Time] has its origins in the life process, in the creativity of the mind, and in social conventions and modes of communication.

—J. T. Fraser (1987: 4)

The denial of time and complexity was central to the cultural issues raised by the scientific enterprise in its classical definition. . . . Today interest is shifting from substance to relation, to communication, to time.

—Ilya Prigogine and Isabelle Stengers (1984: 8)

My title is admittedly provocative.[1] My point is not to conceive of a history shorn of time, nor is it a denial of successivity; it is not an end to history. Instead, I argue that history must embrace the richness and variability of different times that exist throughout our lives, are evident in nonmodern societies and historical writings about them, and have become common in various sciences throughout the twentieth century. To conflate time and chronology is to succumb to what Michel de Certeau calls an alibi—to make "use of time without reflecting on it." Moreover, it is to ignore (as J. T. Fraser, one of the great scholars on time, points out) time as emanating from life (biological and social processes) in favor of a mechanical metric that I will argue has restricted the possibilities of history. The physicist Erwin Schrödinger writes, "We must be prepared to find [the structure of living matter] working in a manner that cannot be reduced to the ordinary laws of physics" ([1944] 1967: 76).[2] And the "denial of time" referred to by Ilya Prigogine and Isabelle Stengers ignores life processes and the structure of living matter by using Newtonian time (now called "classical time" in the sciences). I engage with what they identified as a shifting interest (thirty years ago!) that was moving from substance—the question of what is—to relations and communication. My hope, then, of a history without chronology is an engagement in the multiple times that already exist but have been subsumed or ignored by classical time.

The slowness of the shifting interest identified by Prigogine and Stengers suggests that this is not another fashionable "turn" of academic production; it should be more. To punctuate a need for such an inquiry, I will invoke two major intellectuals, Norbert Elias and Michel Serres. During the last decade of the twentieth century, both argued that we need a different understanding of time; they criticized the prevailing understanding of modern time that we use in everyday life, liberal-capitalism, and scholarship, especially in the humanities and social sciences. This is the time of Newtonian science, an absolute time, external to human society. First, Elias wrote, "An enquiry into 'time', as one may have noticed, is a useful point of departure for the great spring-cleaning that is long overdue. There is always a need for it when an intellectual tradition providing the basic means of orientation within its societies has run its course for several centuries, as ours has from the (so called) Renaissance to the present time" (1992: 93–94). Second, Serres went further, pondering whether progressive time is a persistent myth like the idea that the earth is flat: "But, irresistibly, I cannot help thinking that this idea is the equivalent of those ancient diagrams we laugh at today, which place the Earth at the center of everything, or our galaxy at the middle of the universe, to satisfy our narcissism" (Serres with Latour 1995: 48).

I believe that it is an important moment to take up Elias's challenge for a spring cleaning, and as uncomfortable as Serres's statement might be, he is not an intellectual who can be easily dismissed. Over the past decade or so, scholars have been increasingly discussing time and temporality, and there have been many excellent interventions from which I have benefited. But popularity has also brought what one might call a casual use of the nouns *time* and *temporality*. Too often, despite this move toward a reflective understanding, time and temporality still operate within a notion of absolute time; they merely denote the past, sequence, or history (with all its ambiguity and generality).[3] Tom Boellstorff has pointed out that when anthropology shifted from the hierarchical notion of "Culture" to heterogeneous cultures, it did not also discard the linear time—here, chronology—that undergirded the former (2007a: 30–34). In spite of the occasional and quite powerful inquiries into the problem of time, historians and historical thinking still operate within a framework that predisposes us toward a progressivist and mechanistic desire (or, at minimum, vocabulary); time is still accepted as absolute and natural. Such work reaffirms Certeau's assertion of chronology as the "alibi of time," an unreflected-on category in the discipline of history. Linearity and taxonomy continue—barely modified, at best. We need to do more than change a few nouns and verbs. Unless historians—who should be better equipped?—also decenter chronological time, we still operate within the nineteenth- and twentieth-century frameworks, despite our denials.

I take seriously Eelco Runia's refreshingly honest but damning comment that opens his book: "Sometimes, in unguarded moments, I mutter to my students that 'historians don't think.' . . . the discipline puts a premium on 'sorting things out,' . . . And 'thinking,' I go on, is turning things upside down, is awakening dogs that lie sleeping, is taking things apart, is, in short, willfully making a mess" (2014: xi). This "mess" is thinking anew—questioning existing structures, categories, and methods that have delimited the relation of the present with what is previous (past) as well as anticipated. Elizabeth Ermarth recognizes the potential of the sciences (physical and biological) since Newton for reconsidering our understanding of societies. She writes, "We are surrounded by a world that operates on the principles of quantum theory; we are living in mental worlds that operate on the principles of Newton. . . . But in the subvisible and stellar worlds that surround us, things have changed, and those changes limit the scope and importance both of Newtonian mechanics and of historical thinking" (1992: 10). Thermodynamics, special relativity, quantum mechanics, chronobiology, and cybernetics (complexity) have changed the scientific understanding of time, and these times alter how we understand physical and social processes. To this, we need to add work in cognition that shows that the modes of transmission of information—reading and learning—are but one part of a complex of environment, inherited understanding, and moment.

To ignore more recent understandings of time and cognition gives credence to Serres's indictment that those who deny (or ignore) such scientific understandings are like those who persisted that the earth is flat. In short, our understanding of history is now mythical. We must recognize that continued use of classical time destabilizes those ideas based on it and potentially places them within a mythical mode of thought. Hans Blumenberg warned, "The mythical mode of thought works toward evidentness in the articulation of time; it is able to do this because no one ever asks for its chronology" (1985: 100). If myth is understood as the "practical verities in which the members of the community all believe and live" (Mali 2003: 4), then absolute time has achieved a mythical status in the merger of chronology and history. Blumenberg's mythical mode (our current system) prevails; that conceptual system is linear and regular, and it homogenizes life according to mechanical, linear processes. In its merger with history, chronology has become a social technology that guides and controls us (Mumford 1934). It imposes structure, an ordered mechanical life; it relegates humanistic work—ideas, culture, interpretation, and ethics—to a secondary or lesser value compared to measured work; and it guiles us into thinking that we are better than those before.

The epigraph from Fraser captures the difficulty of posing an inquiry into the relation between time and history. Indeed, time is embedded in life and in modernity; one can go so far as reiterate Marx: "Time is everything, man is nothing; he is at the most the incarnation of time" (quoted in Lukács 1971: 89).[4] Fraser unpacks Marx's statement a bit. Time is embedded in life processes, human reckoning, and cultural practices—that is, the rhythms of all types of organisms as well as the movement of the planets, stars, and galaxies. But there is an ambiguity in Fraser's statement and classical time. Classical time is external to human activity; it is based on Newtonian physics. It has been critical in the formulation of modern systems that guide, organize, order, and control. He points out that we have been using a mechanical metric to order and understand life processes. Another way of conceiving of the difference is that the former necessitates knowledge of the past; history through chronological time has emphasized measurement of categorical units. In contrast, the latter—histories based on times that are from life processes, human cognition, and social activity— becomes an important inquiry that can emphasize human relationality and communication about pasts and their relevance to the present. It allows for multiple forms of evidence, and it suggests narrative strategies to broaden the connections of pasts to some present. I don't think this is a very controversial statement, and many historians have been trying to do so. Yet the problems I outline above persist or are getting worse.

My hope is that in this renewed interrogation of time, scholars, especially historians, first recognize the historicity of chronology as a construct that claims externality and has gained material expression through the clocks, calendars, conceptual forms, and social structures built on them (chapters 1 and 2). Second, I hope they consider how scientific understandings of time that have emerged in the twentieth century might be adapted to reconceive relations of the present and pasts (chapters 3 and 4). A history without chronology is an attempt to offer to history—and the humanistic sciences—a significance that, I believe, they deserve in our lives and our world. It is my attempt to think anew, to make a "mess" (which includes recovery) where we incorporate the multiple times and various temporalities that simultaneously operate in our worlds.

DIGITAL HUMANITIES

Origin stories in history (including my three beginnings in the acknowledgments) are always suspect. Indeed, this is especially a problem of chronological structures; they often disclose the conclusion. Nevertheless, in an essay that will argue for the transparency of process and the efficacy of stories, I should come clean. This project was born out of frustration and liberation. The frustration is my own failure; I have long been interested in the relation between pasts and history (Tanaka 1993), which led me to absolute time and modern society (Tanaka 2004). Yet I recognize that these books failed in my attempt to move beyond a teleological history. Criticism often reinforces the status quo despite reflection and what seems like separation. In writing those books, I was influenced by a number of intellectuals, such as Walter Benjamin, Michel de Certeau, Reinhart Koselleck, Siegfried Kracauer, and Hayden White. I still am. I see my failure, though, as verification of Lev Vygotsky's theory of learning as a zone of proximal development (discussed in chapter 3). As I learn more, I continue to see things they wrote that I had overlooked. I now see those historians as questioning change in history and believe that history is a discipline that does not describe how change happens; the problem of change is discussed in chapter 4. Instead, history describes how societies, nations, and people (biography) became what we know them to be. The very structure of the historical discipline, despite the intent of historians, is conservative. History—whether through acclaim or criticism—reinforces the status quo.

The liberation is in my engagement with digital media and work on new media. I see this book as a project of the digital humanities. This text is certainly not a typical digital humanities product; it is the same long-form (hopefully shortened enough to get the message across) text formatted into a pdf that is printed electronically or on paper. Yet it is a part of the digital humanities because my engagement with digital media has forced me to look anew into how I conceive of and write history. I have been cajoled by what I now call O'Donnell's Law—uptake of digital media increasingly pushes us toward first principles (O'Donnell 2016)—and these first principles seem just to keep coming! Initial use of digital media often enhances current practices, and we have developed new resources, tools, and practices that help us port current analog practices to digital tools and media—for example, electronic dissemination of published work, building digital archives, using mapping software, and adding pictures to narratives.[5] That process, however, gradually raises questions and exposes inconsistencies that lead toward an inquiry into first principles. This process has led me to questions of evidence, of a "fact," how things are categorized, how we connect (or not) those pasts, and finally to the viability of absolute time and absolute space in understanding human activity. These inquiries today range from long-accepted assumptions and categories to considerations of purpose and audience. The opportunity is the possibility of other ways to know about and re-present pasts.

I consider this a digital humanities study in another sense. This book is short; that is intentional. The affordances of digital media encourage scholars to think about audience and how we communicate—it would be ironic (but not uncommon) for a narrative that argues for communication to be monologic. A regular academic monograph on time that covers the topics here would be much longer. I remember a panel at the American Historical Association annual meeting where I interpreted a statement by David Armitage as something like "historians publish to close off discussion." Arguments are carefully argued with much detail, many caveats, and footnotes that show the nuances of the argument. We write, well aware of potential criticisms, and employ preemptive tactics. The result is a carefully argued narrative that is written for a rather tiny audience of fellow specialists.

The advocacy for communication, then, appears in two ways. My hope is that by unleashing history from chronological time, we might again allow history to be also a form of communication about pasts and their relevance to the present, not just a knowledge about the past. Ultimately, I hope to suggest a history that enlarges the past into pasts as well as pasts in the present, allows for multiple forms of evidence, and suggests narrative strategies to broaden the connections of histories to the present. With this book—and its relative brevity, the copyright, and the digital affordances—I hopefully help move academia another step from publishing toward scholarly communication. I had hoped the digital version would incorporate some of the affordances of that media not available in print.[6] The one exciting addition is the opportunity for readers to comment and annotate the text online. This can be a different form of review—not only of books but also of ideas in books. These annotations will be open, and annotations can also be annotated. This can be a way for readers to amend and correct this book (occasional corroboration or praise would be nice!); in my idyllic world where we return to scholarly communication (as contrasted with publishing), the comments would accumulate into another (collectively authored) book. These forms do put into practice some of my key arguments: the value and richness of heterogeneity, the presence of multiple perspectives, and the recognition of differentials in reception/learning. In short, it is not meant to be a book that explains a topic but one that opens up conversation on historical thinking.

Digital media raises another issue for humanistic scholarship, boundaries between objects, information, facts, knowing, and understanding.[7] Throughout the twentieth century, intellectuals have variously questioned the role of the human and cognition in relation to technology. This continues, and despite (or because of) the current obsession with STEM, it remains unresolved (and is not readily resolvable). When we step back, we can learn from work on new media and media archaeology that emphasizes that we are in an era of information inflation (Castillo and Egginton 2017; Huhtamo and Parikka 2011; Smith Rumsey 2016; Standage 2013; and Zielinski 2006). Such work shows that history also has a context. Castillo and Egginton describe inflationary media as a saturation that "is provoking a crisis in how we perceive and understand reality" (2017: 1). They place the first major era subsequent to the spread of the printing press. It led to new ways of seeing, knowing, and experiencing through visual perspective, print culture, and the theater. We are in the second major era, the electronic (beginning with the telegraph), where information (transmitted and stored) is separated from the materiality of what it represents. Information is at the center, and time-space has been continually compressing.[8]

History has an interesting place in this transformation; this will be sketched in chapter 2. On the one hand, it becomes a knowledge system that creates a new reality following the first crisis. Castillo and Egginton point to the nation-state as one of the outcomes of the earlier era of inflationary media (2017: 2). History helped stabilize the uncertainty that followed the spread of print; it created a new reality. Again, this speaks to the conservative tendency of history and its complementarity to printed work, especially the book. On the other hand, from a different vantage point, history can be seen as an early moment in the history of information. Information, according to Claude Shannon, is separated from meaning (Shannon and Weaver 1949); this abstraction is at the heart of the rise of computer science, artificial intelligence, and robotics.[9] History's notion of "facts" can be seen as a predecessor to Shannon's definition. This similarity requires that we look beyond the division between science and the humanities and instead consider this understanding of information as the naturalization of a mechanical system of ordering with its various biases. In the formation of modern history, "facts" are the contents of documents abstracted from their sites of creation and places of meaning. Though perhaps not at the same level as cliometrics, algorithms, and Big Data today, chronological time, nevertheless, is a metric that quantifies. As I show in chapters 1 and 2, it does change what counted as history from a qualitative to quantitative mode of analysis, from individual accounts to knowledge of some collective singular. We must also remember that history itself is being formed at the same time that statistics and probability were entering our knowledge system. Clifford Siskin (2016: 43–77) shows that the words *system* and *history* became common and connected at the end of the eighteenth century.

If history is indeed interested in qualitative accounts, then historical thinking must also be open to qualitative ways of representing pasts; the digital has pushed me to think not only about facts and recorded happenings but also about the similarities between oral and electronic forms of communication (Foley 2012; Herman 2013; Saussy 2016; Standage 2013). Digital media, then, offers us an opportunity to reevaluate the nature and use of past material and whether this flattening is an extension of the "fact" and to use the affordances of technology to present history in multimodal forms, beyond the text (this will be the next part of this project: to "write" examples of a history without chronology). Once we understand the ways that chronology orients us in particular directions away from people and experience and see that the long-form text, the book, complements that emphasis, we can open history to other forms (storytelling and databases) and media (comics and visual forms). My hope is not to make history more enticing (this, I believe, is an important concern) but to write histories that maintain the heterogeneity of and interweave human experiences and sensibilities with "major" events.

Finally, the pervasiveness of digital media; the concern about time, especially the compression into presentism; and the angst of the discipline make this a good moment to think about historical inquiry. While this is not a study that directly addresses the angst of the historical field in the second decade of the twenty-first century, we can see the calls from Elias and Serres to reconsider the way we understand time and the past as their engagement with the second era of information inflation. When we ignore the temporal distance (and presumption of advancement) enforced by dates, we can see a different "reality." For example, we open up the possibility for connections between our current states and pasts, what some are calling "deep time" (Zielinski 2006). Smith Rumsey, for example, chastises us: "Now that we have discovered through empirical science that memory is a dynamic process, strongly inflected by emotion and spatialized in the brain, we have almost caught up with the ancient Greeks" (2016: 171). Certeau, in his encounter with mystics of sixteenth- and seventeenth-century Europe, looks for how they operated during moments when their "reality" changed in a world destabilized from the epistemology that had provided order (1992, 2015). As we know, mystics did not prevail; they were dismissed to a newly created past by a rational and scientific knowledge system—the basis of our modern knowledge system. We too are in transition; we now know that Enlightenment thought has not delivered the promised certainty and truth, and its limitations are increasingly apparent. Our scientific understanding of time has changed, and the gulf with the basis of our modern knowledge system, absolute time, is widening.

Like the mystics, today we are uncertain how to proceed. One reaction might be to wonder whether history is also in danger of becoming, like the mystics that history helped suppress, what

Certeau calls "a proud tradition humbled" (1992: 21). Perhaps there is some danger—but certainly if we don't consider these developments in other fields. Barbara Adam suggests the importance of a better understanding of time: "The explicit focus on time forces us to question established traditions, deprives us of old certainties and presents us instead with potential" (1995: 11). I agree; the recent decline in enrollments and criticism of humanistic inquiry make this a good time to reconsider our relation with pasts and our surroundings. Luce Giard's description of Certeau's goal helps reorient us: "to learn from the past how a social group traverses the desertion of its beliefs and how it might profit from the conditions to which it is subjected in order to invent its liberty and plot out a space of movement" (Giard 2015: ix). In his *Rhythmanalysis*, Henri Lefebvre argues that it is not about the self; he asserts that Descartes's cogito has run its course. Instead, to think is to consider "the diverse relations between human being and the universe" (2004: 17).

In the same way that the absence of chronology helps us see isomorphisms across eras, a "future" can also provide us hints. By future, I am thinking not of what is unknown and ahead of us but of the ideas and understandings of twentieth-century science, many of which have not yet had a significant impact on history, and of affordances offered by digital media.[10] Various theories, laws, and research—for example, on relative time, thermodynamics, biological times, and cognitive science—have suggested the simplicity and even inaccuracy of our current understandings of absolute time, absolute space, and the direct correspondence between object and meaning. Similarities between earlier modes of understanding and recent science raise the question of whether the rationality and science of the past three hundred years is the anomaly rather than the norm. The cognitive scientist David Herman suggests an understanding that connects nonmodern forms of understanding with current cognitive science: "The real becomes not a kernel of factuality to which all world-versions can and should be reduced, but rather a zone of potentiality that refuses reduction to any single account of the way things are" (2013: 149).

OCCLUSIONS AND INVERSIONS

That there is a problem with linear time is certainly not a new contribution; scholars, including historians, have long criticized linearity. Today, more scholars acknowledge a general decline of the idea of "progress" and are critical of teleology, and the hope for some future seems absent, shallow, or short term (Bowker 2014). In German history, David Blackbourn and Geoff Eley (1984) raise the possibility of multiple modernities to get away from the teleology of modernization theory; the writings of Harry Harootunian, Masao Miyoshi, and Tetsuo Najita have been central to the current denial of modernization theory in Japanese history (Najita and Scheiner 1978; Miyoshi and Harootunian 1989, 2002). Of course, the rise of subaltern studies has decentered the imperium (Chatterjee 1986; Chakrabarty 2000), and an important debate calling teleology into question exists in queer studies (Boellstorff 2007a; Traub 2013). There is much more.

Yet despite a long history of criticism, the persistence of linear conceptualizations can be attributed to the way that chronological time is hidden, lurking in the shadows of such critiques. This will be discussed in chapter 2 on history. There are two basic acts that have recurred as I have considered chronology and historical understanding. In my readings on historiography, scholars often use words like *occult, masquerade, specter,* and so on to signify hidden forms that obscure the production and presentation of research. Often, it is unwitting, necessary for the reduction of vast material into relatively short (but still long) books or essays. Even more, there is a powerful structure that maintains the knowledge system, channeling historians to predetermined categories and questions. Thomas Kuhn writes, "In history, more than in any other discipline I know, the finished product of research disguises the nature of the work that produced it" (1977: x).[11] I doubt that history is alone here, but this is a lack of transparency for a discipline that prides itself on documentation (i.e., footnotes).

When I first encountered Kuhn's comment, I thought about the primary material—the documents, stories, details, contingency, and discoveries—that is a part of the pleasure of research but is written out of our (often soporific) monographs. On the one hand, the criteria of documentation and the "fact" delimits and often eliminates experience, emotions, and the senses from modern history; the erasure of individual details, sensibilities, and their accounts is a part of the shift to a modern history. I recognize that numerous historians have been trying to reinstate many of these human sensibilities for decades but, I argue, have been restricted by a structure and methodology institutionalized over the past two hundred years. With the digital technologies, expanded archives, creativity of many historians, *and* multiple times, we can bring the heterogeneity of human experience as well as the variability of change back into history. In chapter 3, I argue that an understanding of heterogeneous pasts aids in recovering human sensibilities as a part of history.

I now read Kuhn's statement to reflect a more sinister problem, a hidden (yet in the open for all to see) framework—chronological time.[12] The difficulty of unpacking modern time is evident in Walter Benjamin's critique of this empty, homogeneous time (1968b: 262). Benjamin's words have been popularized by Benedict Anderson's reuse of modern time as empty and homogeneous, thereby providing a critique—but one that reconfirms absolute time.[13] While absolute time homogenizes (while recognizing unevenness), it is certainly not empty. It is only so if one overlooks the politics of its making—that is, the history of time and the history of history. When this recurs, the politics of time disappear into the particulars of becoming. This notion of empty is the working of chronology as an "alibi of time."

Chronology emphasizes succession, the chaining of things one after another. It fosters a language of accumulation and replacement. Inherited knowledge and practices, *historia magistra vitae* (history as life's teacher), were reclassified into some collective singular—primarily the fragmentation of worlds into nation-states—while chronological time provided the structure for new arrangements, reclassification, and manipulations.[14] In twentieth-century language, it is the organization of diverse places into the international order as well as a universal understanding of the world. In a different language, it is the ordering of heterogeneity into one homogenized system. For example, Steven Shapin describes the common notion of the Scientific Revolution as a rhetoric of "wholesale rejection and replacement" of new for old or modern over traditional (1996: 65–80). Chronological time is behind the rhetoric of many Enlightenment intellectuals who denigrate the old as a ploy to elevate their "new" ideas. It complements the presumption that humans (or, more accurately at that time, men) through reason effect change; they are not beholden to God, gods, or nature. And from this activity, societies can move from an originary state to an increasingly improved state to civilization—progress. We should not facilely follow the rhetoric, which is clearly an ideology (but our ideology).[15] Chronology is the "hidden" foundation that enables the facile argument that the new is better than the old. Instead, this transformation was less a "new" that replaced an "old" and instead an inversion of the relation between inherited forms and the present.[16]

In *The Mystic Fable*, Certeau suggests that this emphasis on succession occludes other processes, especially that of reassignment and inversion. He argues that a way to understand and move beyond this linearity is to recognize the inversions that occurred and the need to historicize our research—that is, the very frameworks we operate within—and dehistoricize the objects of study.[17] This is perhaps an odd statement for a discipline that considers itself reflective about historicism, historicity, historiography, and so on: the various ways that research and interpretation inflect the past. Certeau's statement is a recognition of the ways that our current scholarly practices, though historical and performative, have been accepted as natural and objective. This performativity is hidden in chronological time through the use of inversion but masked historically as succession. Inversion is a process that was central to the formulation of chronological time. By recognizing inversions masked through a framework of linear replacement and an ideology of progress (or development), we too can employ inversion to move away from the straightforward chaining of things as succession or replacement (from old to new).[18]

The trope of inversion recognizes that at the foundation of this adaptation of absolute time is the shift toward a structure that prioritizes change and movement over stability, and in that transformation existing practices and ways of knowing were inverted, not necessarily replaced. Inherited knowledge and practices were reclassified into new categories; primarily, the dead past or old things and worlds were fragmented or consolidated into nation-states. Chronological time provided the temporal order for new arrangements, reclassification, and manipulations. What had been a relational condition now became fixed; spatial units, using absolute space, were organized into a hierarchical order based on absolute time and naturalized through temporal narratives of becoming.

This Newtonian time inverts the norm of stability from one of repetition and recurrence to change and motion. This move is brilliant. Diverse times (that are largely cyclical and recurrent and that exist biologically, physically, and socially) are emplotted as some condition before or closer to nature (again, repetition). But this linear system depends on the unending recurrence of past and present. This separated past becomes a boundary marker, a way to contrast the present to what is dead and outmoded, thereby "proving" progress. It takes a relational and heuristic description and fixes the relationship as a function of time. Serres describes this process that reinforces oneself: "The advantage of having at one's borders an hereditary enemy is immense. So is that of having a dialectic in one's logic. It allows one to remain comfortably within the concept, never to contemplate multiplicity" (Serres 1995: 83–84). Repetition is inverted from the stability of the society to the stability of the system. The separation of old from new becomes the repeated foundational process for the maintenance of the modern.

Chronological time also changes what we know and what we look for. Certeau argues this new history makes time, via chronology, a way of classifying data; it creates scriptural tombs.[19] These "tombs" have been an important way to order the heterogeneous societies and new forms of objects being discovered since the fifteenth century. Time becomes a quantitative measure to determine distance, difference, and relations. Each place, object, event, and document becomes a unique point on a grid of time and space. Time establishes a distance between events, a sequencing for making connections, and a way to mark repetition or recurrence. It simultaneously establishes a value system—motion is better than stasis, linearity better than repetition, and new better than old—while depending on that which it denigrates.

BEGINNING: HISTORIES WITHOUT CHRONOLOGY

This did not start out as an ambitious project—to change how we think about time and history. But my historical training took over; historians follow the evidence. My evidence, reframed by the digital humanities, took me into the ways that humans have conceived of and use time. This inquiry ran into history—that is, the ways that our particular understandings of pasts have remained stable as understandings around them have changed. As I continue, my readings extend beyond the discipline. I must admit, I enjoy reading accounts of the Macy Conferences on cybernetics, whose purpose Gregory Bateson described as "the biggest bite out of the fruit of the Tree of Knowledge that mankind has taken in the last 2000 years" (Pias 2016: 11), or Lefebvre's

Rhythmanalysis, which proposes "to found a science, a new field of knowledge: the analysis of rhythms" (2004: 3). I find these to be earlier versions of the quotes from Elias and Serres at the beginning of this introduction. I have constantly been reminded as I continued this work that despite the brilliant work of scholars before me, historians tend not to appropriate material and ideas unless it suits the discipline. For a discipline that is strongly empirical, this is at best ironic. It confirms Blumenberg's statement that "no one ever asks for [time's] chronology" (1985: 100). Chapters 1 and 2 ask.

This raises an interesting tension in this short book. I am not nearly as confident (nor able) as Bateson or Lefebvre. My goal has been to provoke discussion in the historical discipline. Yet by pushing to expand how historians approach pasts, it connects to historical thinking that is tied to so many fields of the humanities and social sciences. I see this as the need for and centrality of historical thinking, of history in our contemporary world.

The digital humanities has also offered hope that there are other ways to do things. This, of course, is a frustration, as so much of digital media (and, even more, technology) is used to reinforce the existing system and conceptual structures. So be it; it can also offer ways outside of the silos. But to do so, we must both embrace and interrogate basic structures. It is not that hard to see the possibilities, once we start looking for understandings of pasts based on heterogeneity and nonlinearity (chapters 3 and 4). It is the basis of human life and societies (in Fraser's words [1987], life processes, the creativity of mind, and social activity); it is in science—the role of perspective, location, and situatedness; and it is biology—the ways that time is internal to organisms and communities of practice. These reinforce a comment by psychologist Sam Wineberg that historical thinking "goes against the grain of how we ordinarily think" (2001: 7). In short, heterogeneity, multiple times, and complexity are around us but are obscured by a knowledge system that emerged to control this heterogeneity through an orderly and homogenizing system. The potential is to recover these human practices and sensibilities.

In the second half of the book, I explore how we can attend to this world of multiples—heterogeneity of pasts and multiple times—to understand how people use and appropriate pasts in their present. This statement can also describe history today, but the key difference is in the multiple, which inverts time from an externality to a part of human activity prior to categorization, and in the need for other ways to connect these multiples—for example, through conjunction (Braudel 1980) or coincidence (Boellstorff 2007a) rather than successive emplotment.

In chapter 3, I reconceive of how we represent pasts, allowing for a preservation of the heterogeneity of forms prior to categorization into homogenizing categories. First, we need to reengage with history again to dehistoricize what we study, placing things, people, and objects back into their "contemporary configuration." This effort to use the situatedness of things is in contrast to the way that objects have been abstracted by using dates along a universalizing chronology to enable separation and reinsertion. When we do so, we find layered and complex interactions that help us see the myriad influences on people, ideas, and things as they interact and transform. Second, to historicize our research is to pay attention to what Fraser (1987) calls histories, a notion of history as a place of local knowledge where diversity is preserved.

Chapter 4 explores ways that such activities connect—sharing, interaction, relations, adaptation, and transformation—or don't with other communities of activity. The goal is to think anew of relationality and emergence, what historians usually reduce to change. But change is not a truism ("change across time"), something that happens or does not in relation to movement. Indeed, these units emerge from repetition, and if we accept entropy or homeostasis, change is much more various: it can be a part of the process of maintenance, of a dynamic equilibrium; it can be decay, occurring at different rates depending on the internal time of the activity and happening through various layers both in and not in connection with others. These histories are independent, coterminous, or parallel each other and exist within, alongside, or autonomous from a universalistic, linear time, what Fraser (1987) calls (and fears) the world-time compact.

Finally, for the practice of history in the digital age, with increasingly instant accessibility to information about pasts, the role of the historian as expert of "facts" during a particular time and space of the past becomes decreasingly important. Instead, the historian, whose strength has always been interpretation of myriad pasts, becomes highlighted. Again, we should remember Droysen's sage comment that is reducible to a meme: "Facts are stupid without interpretation."[20] The inversion we need is to consider facts as what they are—information. Information can be abstracted—Shannon's bits separated from meaning—or "facts" can be abstracted from the situated conditions. Information can also be ideas, things, memory, and inherited knowledge that people use to create understanding, make decisions, and convince others. As Paul Duguid and John Seely Brown (2000) argue, information has a social life. Instead of knowing, the historian who can make sense of data—judgment, manipulation, interpretation, and rhetoric—becomes even more important in the digital age.

History is much too important a field to be limited to a knowledge system of places and things. It will be needed and can be even more important (my hope) in the future. I will end by invoking Prigogine and Stengers (1984), a physicist and a philosopher of science on complexity, and Certeau, a historian of sixteenth-century mystics. In their epigraph the former see how our understanding shifts from objects and being to relations and communication; the latter uses this as an intellectual quest, to "reorganize places for people to communicate" (1992: 165).

CHAPTER ONE

TIME HAS A HISTORY

With regard to authors, it is a mark of supreme cowardice to give unlimited credit to authors and to deny its rights to Time, the author of authors and thus of all authority. For truth is rightly called the daughter of time and not of authority.

—Sir Francis Bacon ([1620] 2004: 69)

Absolute, true, and mathematical time, of itself, and from its own nature flows equably without relation to anything external, and by another name is called duration.

—Sir Isaac Newton ([1687] 1995: 13)

What for others are deviations are, for me, the data which determine my course.—On the differentials of time (which, for others, disturb the main lines of the inquiry), I base my reckoning.

—Walter Benjamin (1999: 456)

Time is a difficult topic for historians. I remember an occasion when I was in the history department and I commented that—alluding to Koselleck—modern history not only is in time but also operates through it (1985: 246). This generated a rather snide comment from a colleague, a disgust with "theory," which is the only explanation for something that needlessly complicates what is so obvious and commonsensical as time. This reaction adheres to the words of Bacon in the epigraph without recognizing the power that Bacon bequeaths to time. This conflation of chronology with absolute time parallels what Lefebvre identifies as a double illusion in the simplification of space to absolute space—that of transparency and reality (1991: 26–29). This refusal to entertain the possibility of times other than chronological time is a refusal to inquire into the system that guides our ways of knowing and being. Even more, as I will show in this and the next chapter, the historicity of chronological time is empirically verifiable using normative historical methods.[1] A refusal to accept this history is the denial of the very empiricism that this former colleague espoused. It is the kind of thinking that leads Runia to mutter, "Historians don't think" (2014: xi).

Thankfully, more and more scholars are attuned to the many forms of time—and indeed, *times*—that human understanding and reckoning of time are historical, and that history is a key determinant of the social and cultural makeup of communities. A rich literature on time—its history and multiple forms—exists and needs to be brought into our writing of history and, more broadly, historical thinking.[2] Failure to recognize this scholarship has allowed history (and the historical thinking it fosters) to reach at least two contradictory conditions, both of which can be called "fatally confused" (Bastian 2012).[3] First, echoing Castillo and Egginton and Rumsey Smith on information inflation, we seem to be reaching a moment where our knowledge system and understanding of the world are decreasingly able to account for the vast increase of information available today. Bigger and cheaper storage devices only solve a small part of the problem. Bastian provocatively suggests that our continued use of Newtonian time makes us oblivious to the fact that nature (long considered stable and unchanging) is changing faster than modern society. This confusion can be extended to other realms. Sheldon Wolin argues that "political time is out of synch with the temporalities, rhythms, and pace governing economy and culture" (1997). Ermarth writes, "The tools of thought inherited from modernity are increasingly at odds with our personal and practical situations and thus indicate a growing and even urgent need for consideration and re-consideration of what the changes demonstrated imply for long-familiar assumptions about identity, time, causality, creativity and politics" (2011: 3). The list of examples of this fatal confusion, the disjunction between observation and inherited notions of reality, is growing.

Second, we must accept the possibility that history, the field of knowledge that has ordered the world, is now mythical.[4] I will discuss this more below, but at this point, it is enough to point out that since the turn of the twentieth century, the science on which absolute time was based now exists amid newer understandings— for example, Einstein's special relativity, the laws (especially second) of thermodynamics, chronobiology, and quantum theory. Absolute time is now called "classical time" (not to be confused temporally with the classical period of history), signifying the presence of other notions of time more akin to modern science. Modern history operates on an outmoded notion of time, though it is commonly believed, especially socioculturally. But now that notion is one of several, which, if employed, must at minimum be defended rather than assumed.

Today, more than ever, we need to evaluate the very structure of historical understanding—to discern science, myth, and ideology. This issue is not "new." The examples cited above suggest also that the disconnect between scientific time and chronological time existed throughout the twentieth century, if not earlier. As science was moving away from absolute time, the international and nation-state systems, the social sciences, and the humanities developed through absolute time. This recalls Elias's plea for a "spring cleaning." An initial step toward a richer understanding of how humans use pasts to make sense of their world is rather simply stated: to bring times into histories rather than describing history in time. There are many different times: the physical happenings, rhythms of chronobiology, and rhythms of assemblages both small and large. Each of these times might have several temporalities within each. These times have been overshadowed, or "colonized," by linear, progressive time that Geoffrey Bowker (2014) has described as a "sociotechnical imaginary" time. This is our modern time; it will not be easy to reformulate this time, nor am I advocating its elimination. In the sciences, absolute time coexists with relative and quantum times. My goals are not critique and replacement (which often results in supporting the status quo), but I suggest the multiple ways we can understand times that place what Benjamin in the epigraph calls "differentials of time" as constituent elements of our lives rather than as emplotments along a universalizing sociotechnical imaginary.

Before we can move to these differentials of time, it is essential to outline, briefly, a history of time—that is, to show that our current understanding is social, not natural.[5]

NONMODERN TIMES

Scholars who have studied nonmodern people and places (ancient, medieval, and non-Western) are aware of the different ways that time has been reckoned. When one looks, there are many fine historical accounts of times in ancient, medieval, and early modern places. Anthropologists have long described different understandings of time in the cultures they studied.[6] Much of the information that follows in the first section is familiar; my goal is not to present something new but to suggest other ways people have reckoned time when absolute time was not the metric for order and becoming. There were, simply, other ways of understanding, many of which can be found (or would be helpful) today.

Prior to the modern period, and in places not dominated by abstract time, time is episodic, local, uneven, and irregular. Some days are more favorable than others. Indeed, calendars were used not to show the passage of time but to mark place, significance, and meaning.[7] In post-Reformation Europe, Friday was "thought unlucky for any venture, whether marrying, making a journey or even cutting one's nails," and in Yorkshire (England), servants considered Monday an unlucky day to change employer (Thomas 1971: 619). The luni-solar calendar in Tokugawa society (Japan) was not a grid of passing days but an information sheet of major and minor months, divinatory signs, and auspicious/inauspicious days. The magnificent clock at the Strasbourg cathedral includes an automated astrolabe, a perpetual calendar, a carillon, a virgin holding the Christ child, a mechanical cock that flapped its wings and crowed, and "a tablet showing the body parts and their correlation with the zodiac for the favorable and unfavorable times for bloodletting" (Haber 1975: 399–400). Such uneven time remains: our legacy of "superstitions" like Friday the 13th are an example, and in Japan today, many calendars (Gregorian) still mark the auspicious (*taian*) or inauspicious (*butsumetsu*) days (now important for deciding celebratory events like weddings). In some working-class communities, the regularity of the everyday is as much or more valued than the developmental time of middle-class societies (Perovic 2017; Negt and Kluge 1993).

In medieval and early modern societies, mechanical time was secondary to social time. What we now see as exquisite detail and craftsmanship on early clocks exhibited socially meaningful information.[8] Derek de Solla Price argues, "The first great clocks of medieval Europe were designed as astronomical showpieces, full of complicated gearing and dials to show the motions of the Sun, Moon and planets, to exhibit eclipses, and to carry through the involved computations of the ecclesiastical calendar. As such they were comparable to the orreries of the 18th century and to modern planetariums; that they also showed the time and rang it on bells was almost incidental to their main function" (1959: 86). In other words, the positions of celestial bodies were more important than the time of the day. The movement of the stars was a way to discern auspicious and inauspicious days, weather, the growth of crops, and medical information about the human body. The "hour" of the day, the temporal hour, was also uneven, divided into equal units of daylight and night. Many early mechanical clocks (fourteenth-century Europe) did not have a minute hand, and if they did, it needed to be periodically corrected using a sundial. In East Asia after the Jesuits introduced clocks, these mechanical devices became markers of wealth and prestige. In Edo society (seventeenth- to nineteenth-century Japan), craftsmen added a second folio so that these status symbols could follow the temporal hour. Mechanical time had to be adjusted to social time.

Previous reckoning systems for the year varied widely. Medieval Jews used three chronological systems: the era of creation, the era of the destruction of the Second Temple, and the Seleucid era (Yerushalmi [1982] 1996: 41). Our current chronology, the linear reckoning of years as BC/AD or BCE/CE, is relatively recent, becoming the principal system in the seventeenth century.[9] Dionysus Exiguus first proposed in 532 a reckoning system, beginning with the birth of Christ (anno Domini) as year one.[10] Dionysus's system was not dominant but coexisted with numerous others. Time systems were local. Local events, not abstract years, served as the key markers. The olympiads provided a regular marker for dating the year in ancient Greece, the indiction was a common system in the Roman world, and the Bible provided another.

Chronological reckoning came with the Enlightenment. At the end of the sixteenth century, Joseph Scaliger formulated a Julian period, a singular, continuous, and linear time of 7,980 years. Christ's birth within this system was year 4713. In the seventeenth century, Domenicus Petavius moved chronology closer to an absolute time by removing time from religion. He wrote, "Chronology indeed inquires after one thing, by what signs and marks each thing may be arranged in its years and times" (Wilcox 1987: 205). Nevertheless, Petavius retained Dionysus's birth of Christ—not, he claimed, for its religious significance but as a conventional point of reference. Petavius's major (and lasting) contribution was to add years before Christ to fill out the chronology.[11] In the western Pacific, when new leaders sought to create the nation-state of Japan following the Meiji *ishin* (the revolution in 1868), they adopted two systems, a linear sequence beginning from the ascension of the mythical emperor Jinmu and a modified *nengo* that counted years by emperors' reigns.[12] The subsequent rendering of previous events and the temporal systems of other societies according to Petavius's timeline is a translation into this Enlightenment system.

Clearly time was not central to the organization and makeup of these societies, but it would be a mistake to conclude from this brief outline that nonmodern places (ancient, medieval, non-West) did not understand or were "indifferent to time" (Gurevich 1985: 151).[13] Jeffrey J. Cohen argues that time was very important, but it was not the mechanical, absolute time of our world. He writes, "Medieval writers were just as enamored of investigating the complexities of both *temporality* (the nature and working of time) and *history* (the transformation of time into narrative) as recent theorists have been" (2003: 2). Cohen, like so many scholars of medieval and early modern periods, as well as those of non-Western places, is reacting to the propensity in history to conclude facilely that earlier periods were not as sophisticated as ours, the modern.[14] One need merely peruse Bede's reckoning to see incredible sophistication on lunar and solar cycles, sacred time, and sociopolitical times. The Mayan calendar is a remarkable system comprehensible today only to specialists. Calendar keeping was a prestigious role; controlling time bore significant power. In Edo society, the imperial court, the *bakufu* (government), and some domains employed astronomical scholars to determine the calendars. The major concern among scholars in Christian Europe was determining the date of Easter. Adolph Holl discerned a new desire to "know the time" around twelfth- and thirteenth-century Europe (cited in Nowotny 1994: 16). This desire was partly fueled by an expanded world in which merchants needed to calculate the costs of distant trade. This increased concern for time began an interaction between space and time that has continued through the spatial compression we experience today.

As the above suggests, time need not be a metric to emplot and organize but a way to understand the world that surrounds us. It was (is) a mysterious and powerful world. The historian Aron J. Gurevich writes, "Both space and time are axiologically and emotionally charged: time and space can be good or evil . . . there is a sacral time, a time to make merry, a time for sacrifice, a time for the re-enactment of the myth . . . and . . . there are sacred places or whole worlds subject to special forces" (1985: 29). Interestingly, time is something to pay attention to. It is internal to society, something that one can change: "Time in archaic society is not something outside people, unrelated to their lives and doings. On the contrary, it is something within them, and therefore it is possible to influence its course and even its quality" (103). Today, in contrast, because we operate with time as an externality, we feel caught up by time (Eriksen 2001; Levy 2007; Rushkoff 2013).

One of the hardest ideas for us to grasp is that the constant passage of time—past, present, and future—did not always exist as we understand it today. Ancient Greeks perceived and experienced their world "as remaining at rest, or as orbiting in a great circle" (Gurevich 1985: 31). Repetitive time was in the contemporaneous, while movement was the transition toward eternity. Gurevich writes, "Man did not feel himself to be existent in time; 'to be' for him meant 'to abide,' not 'to be in the process of becoming'" (133). The passage that did exist (history) was devolution toward the end, then renewal. Jacques Le Goff notes that the prevailing idea in medieval Europe was *mundus senescit*, "the world grows old" (Le Goff 2015: 8). This connection with passage and decay was also built into the Confucian Mandate of Heaven, which calls for the overturning of incompetent governance, and farther east, in what is now Japan, renewal was allowed within imperial reigns. What we today call the past—things that happened and are prior and distinct—was not distant nor different; inherited ideas that were important enough to be retained were of the present. In a world that grows old, the future as something better did not exist. In his discussion of the famous early historians Polybius and Sima Qian, Gurevich writes that "history was no more than the eternal return in a prescribed order of the same political forms" (1985: 33). Anticipation of something to come, of course, existed. But for something to be anticipated, it had to be based on some experience. Some peoples whose horizon is based on experiential knowledge point behind themselves to indicate the future (Nunez and Sweetser 2006; Nowotny 2008: 1). This directionality recalls Benjamin's interpretation of Paul Klee's "Angelus Novum," in which the angel is being blown to the future while looking backward at an ever-increasing accumulation of destruction (1968b: 257–58).

In these places, iterative acts of recurrence, where knowledge is handed down through memory and oral traditions, can be a way of maintaining a particular place. Gurevich described time during the ancient period as "spatialized"—that is, dependent on space and environment: "Ancient man saw past and present stretching round him, in mutual penetration and clarification of each other. An event which took place previously and an event happening now can be perceived by the archaic consciousness as manifestations in one and the same plane, extended in one and the same temporal duration" (1985: 29). In these worlds, repetition invokes either a sense of stability through constancy or a connection to some eternal ideal.

This certainly does not mean that these societies were static. Repetition and redundancy can be conservative (place-making and maintenance); it can also lead to variation and change.[15] For example, in Japan, the architecture of the Ise Shrine, because its periodic rebuilding depended on the memory, skill, and materials available, evolved over the millennia despite its reputation for originality (Isozaki 2006). We know that stories, fables, and epics changed as they were disseminated, a mode of preservation. Today as well, such repetitive time from chronobiology, habits and customs, and repetitive labor are a constituent part of modern society (Young 1988; Sharma 2014). Recent scholarship shows that as economic processes become more efficient, we increasingly depend on cyclical, commodified labor. We see this process in the elevation of subcontracting work in Japanese factories; Sarah Sharma has shown how participation in the hypermanaged and efficient clock time of global capitalism depends heavily on cyclical and on-demand labor; and Lilly Irani describes how a technological startup increasingly turns to subcontracting of mundane tasks to maintain its rapid momentum (Sharma 2014; Irani 2019).

Koselleck's notion of two forms of social organization—spaces of experience and horizons of expectations—is useful while also showing the limitation of categories that derive from stability and motion. Nonmodern places are characteristic of spaces of experience. The emphasis is in the present past; depth did (and does) exist in an "eternal present." The space of experience is one where locale, not time, provided a different understanding of depth and connectivity. In such places where recursive acts are the norm, perfection might be the goal, but change was often seen as deterioration— humans could not replicate what the gods or God created: *mundus senescit*. The horizon of expectations is more common to bourgeois society: the future made present. It is directed toward the not-yet as something to be revealed (Koselleck 1985: 267–88). We will be moving to abstract time shortly. Koselleck argues that these forms are successive and/or coexistent, and in his later writings, he argues for a layering of time (*Zeitschichten*; 2018: 3–9).

At this point, it is important to decouple descriptions of nonmodern places from chronology. This tendency to linearity has been a principal reason that these accounts are easily overlooked. Mobility (change) and stability are conditions of communities and are not characteristics of the modern/premodern. An important difference is in the placement of time. When time is internal, various aspects of the activity remain present; both change and repetition are evident. When time is externalized—that is, with the discovery of absolute time—it becomes possible to obscure, hide, or ignore various parts of the process. This principally happens in two ways. First is the practice of translating (or, more accurately, transmuting) times to modern, chronological time as if it is a mechanical act. Second, and more important, is that these accounts of nonmodern places are located as some temporal condition of the inferior or unsophisticated. In anthropology, Fabian calls this allochronism, a denial of coevalness where the culture, even though contemporary, is primitive and foreign (1983). In nonmodern histories, it is of places that are past and different. A description of the way that these acts reinforce chronological time will be discussed in chapter 2.

"ABSOLUTE, TRUE, AND MATHEMATICAL TIME"[16]

Our modern time—that is, the notions that time is external (absolute), constantly flows linearly (true), and is regular (mechanical)—came into being gradually. I will only offer a general overview, enough to make my point; there are several fine accounts of this transformation to an absolute time (see, for example, Adam 2004; Elias 1992; Fraser 1987; Nowotny 1994; Toulmin and Goodfield 1965; Wilcox 1987). This shift toward abstract time occurred in Europe, and universal time was formulated there. Le Goff (1980) writes about the transformation of time between the twelfth and fifteenth centuries as a difficult effort to deal with the coexistence of natural time (the various cycles of seasons, stars, planets, sun, and moon), professional time (measurement for trade and transactions), and supernatural time (religious and supernatural understandings).[17] By the nineteenth century, absolute time reoriented these times: natural time was relegated to an originary status, professional time used absolute time to reconceive social processes and value, and supernatural time was relegated to the past.

By the sixteenth century, changes were manifold. The break-down of the feudal order involved the spread of printing presses, the formation of states, the discovery of the New World, the rise of merchants, and the Protestant Reformation (Shapin 1996: 119–65; Standage 2013: 48–63). This crisis contributed to a per-ceived need for order, what Carolyn Merchant argues was the "fundamental social and intellectual problem for the seventeenth century" ([1980] 1989: 192). In this search, absolute time was one alternative. Mystics explored a mystic science in the sixteenth and seventeenth centuries (Certeau 1992, 2015), universal history recognized multiple chronologies (Jordheim, forthcoming), and self-organization—a distant predecessor to complex systems—gained ground in the early eighteenth century (Sheehan and Wahrman 2015).

Newton brought together a series of ideas that culminated in the late seventeenth century—in particular, the desire to under-stand mathematically the mechanical operations of the world.[18] In the epigraphs from Bacon and Newton, the assertions are seductively simple and seem obvious to us today. Bacon inverted authority from the past (God) to the present (science), and New-ton's often-quoted declarative statement of time removed time from human activity to an externality. It has its own regularity, flows, and can be measured, creating duration.[19] The order that is made possible through *Principia* is one in which the world can be rendered as matter and material that, subject to universal laws, can be ordered, known, and manipulated mathematically (i.e., quantitatively). But this notion of time shifts scholarship from relations—understanding, experience, and sensation—to knowl-edge about material objects, their movement, and how they com-pare. Prigogine and Stengers write, "The ambition of Newtonian science was to present a vision of nature that would be universal, deterministic, and objective inasmuch as it contains no reference to the observer, complete inasmuch as it attains a level of descrip-tion that escapes the clutches of time" (1984: 213).

The clutches of time of Prigogine and Stengers is the life processes, the creativity, and the social conventions that Fraser (1987) calls for in the epigraph to the introduction. The escape from this time was to remove time (and scientific laws) from human activity and sensibility and turn it into an externality that is ostensibly neutral for all measurable knowledge. Barbara Adam succinctly describes the strength of Newtonian time: "[Time] is linked to a number and the measure of motion, duration, and rate" (1990: 51). Chronological time is now hidden in plain sight, yet the transformation is profound. On the one hand, the scientists, who know the laws and abstract principles, become the omniscient, neutral observer. On the other hand, it transposes all previous connections of time in society away from experience. Fraser writes, "Gone were the attempts to relate time to the motion of the stars (as proposed by Plato), to the 'number of motion' (Aristotle), to the mind (Augustine), to the world and mankind (Averroës), or to life and feeling. Time became a type of universal order that existed by and in itself, regardless of what happened in time" (1987: 41). Fraser is describing the transition from various understandings of finite worlds where stability begins in fixity (creation) to an infinite universe always in motion.

This is the escape from the "clutches of time." Time changes from activity and sensibility of humans to a mechanical, clock-like movement, a putatively neutral time that is bidirectional and turns motion into a default condition. Newtonian time establishes a single system that will be used to unify the many reckoning systems into one system that, though formulated in Europe, is presented as universal. That is, the world becomes renderable mechanically and mathematically.

CLOCK TIME

A central, or perhaps the most important, device and symbol that fostered this transition to mechanical time is the clock. The impact of the clock cannot be overemphasized. Mumford states matter-of-factly, "The clock, not the steam-engine, is the key-machine of the modern industrial age" (1934: 14).[20] Indeed, it predates absolute time. Bells from thirteenth-century Europe and Tokugawa Japan and then public clocks in fourteenth-century Europe slowly began to order the work day (Le Goff 1980; Frumer 2018; Glennie and Thrift 2009). Clock time as a common system to synchronize large groups of people became widespread with industrialization (Le Goff 1988; Gurevich 1985; Thompson 1967).

Perhaps the greatest significance of the clock for my discussion is as a metaphor, a machine. It was a part of the transition of knowledge from a world of gods, spirits, or animistic powers to the laws that we now see as a part of science (Shapin 1996; Merchant [1980] 1989). Johannes Kepler writes, "My aim in this is to show that the machine of the universe is not similar to a divine animated being, but similar to a clock." (quoted in Shapin 1996: 33). The artificial, which is man-made, was no longer an inferior version of the world. This image represents a particular notion of the machine as humankind's ability to exploit energy and to mechanize (i.e., develop) productive enterprises. The clock dissociates time from human activity and reinforces the idea that time is independent and measurable.

Within this metaphor of a clock, both a progressive time and a repetitive time coexist; indeed, they depend on each other (Bowker 2014). Up to this point, time was isotropic; Newtonian time could move in both directions. Clock time suggests forward motion, while cycles of the hour and day reinforce repetition and redundancy. The calendar does the same through the lunar cycle, seasons, and solar cycle. It is important to point out that clock time reoriented life and work around mechanically repetitive, not lived processes (Thompson 1967). Much has been written about the transformation of industrial society around clock time. Mumford writes, "Abstract time became the new medium of existence. Organic functions themselves were regulated by it: one ate, not upon feeling hungry, but when prompted by the clock: one slept, not when one was tired, but when the clock sanctioned it" (1934: 17). Clock time has become so naturalized that social and organic functions have merged with mechanical time. It dominates our modern world to the extent that efforts to resolve our imbrication in time have usually been to become more efficient, further entangling us in absolute time. Leisure too acts as a respite from regulated work life, yet it replicates the structure and regularity of clock time (Elias 1986).[21]

Applying this idea of time occurred gradually, and it was not until the eighteenth and nineteenth centuries that it was widely accepted. Change does not occur linearly; linear narratives often obscure the multiple strands of transition.[22] During a transformation, there is the maintenance of inherited forms; unsuccessful efforts to create an alternate understanding; multiple, parallel ideas; dismissal of novel ideas that only later become recognized as significant; and, of course, the great figures (Bacon and Newton) who bring together many of the parallel and competing ideas. A linear time did not replace cyclical time. These are not antithetical; repetitive time is a constituent part of absolute time. Shapin writes that even during the age of Newton and Boyle, "the idea of linear, cumulative intellectual progress was still novel and not widely accepted" (1996: 74). My point here is that progressive time is a particular understanding of absolute time where the inversion, repetitive time, though central, has been backgrounded in order to highlight progressive time. This is evident in the epigraph from Bacon in which he inverted the relationship between repetition (authority) and linearity (time).

One can cite many intellectuals who helped develop and spread this idea. At the end of the seventeenth century, John Locke described the human in developmental terms.[23] In his *Some Thoughts Concerning Education*, Locke used a metaphor of wax tablets to describe the education of children. That is, children were blank slates that needed to be schooled so that they would develop into proper gentlemen.[24] Jean Jacques Rousseau went further in his *Emile*, arguing that children learn and develop as they grow—it is a natural process—and deviation, even an acceleration of learning, leads to precocious, malformed adults. In both cases the human is now born with limited abilities and must develop, and this development depends on upbringing and education. Development becomes the structure to understand physiological growth, subsuming the organic, cyclical process.[25] Moreover, in the eighteenth century, the emergence of mathematics and probability offered a new way to look at patterns, and a sense of a future gained substance.[26] Actuary tables and the lottery were two early applications of this new predictive form of knowledge. Individual experience is subsumed into a larger, abstract whole, and pasts—the data extracted to create the aggregates—are used to point to a future.

Nature too was discovered to fit within absolute time. During the late eighteenth and early nineteenth centuries, people began to question the age of the earth, separating its creation from the biblical account. Comte de Buffon, using the contemporary understanding of physics, calculated that the earth was approximately seventy-five thousand years old, not the four thousand years commonly accepted from the Bible (Toulmin and Goodfield 1965: 142–50). Charles Lyell's *Principles of Geology* built on Buffon and many others to demonstrate that the earth has a history that is independent of the Bible (or other creation myths).[27] By the nineteenth century, there was a general agreement in the idea of progress. To reinforce this as a part of the sociotechnical imaginary, it is an idea (desire) attached to time, giving it direction. Koselleck (2002: 229–30) points out that progress becomes a historical agent: "progress of time." It gained status as a collective singular that combines numerous experiences; and by the nineteenth century, it became nominal: "progress itself."

To complete this brief story, the unification of the globe at the official level around a universal time took a big step in 1884 at the International Meridian Conference. The conference adopted a single global time of twenty-four time zones with Greenwich as the prime meridian. Here, again, was the interrelation of an expanded world and its connection to time. The Harrison H4 chronometer won the Longitude Prize for an accurate chronometer that helped captains of ships reckon longitude. The railroad necessitated a time synchronized according to a single standard, and the proposal for the twenty-four time zones emerged from standard railroad time in the US (Bartky 2000). The meridian conference, in a sense, brought Kepler's desire to fruition—the clock synchronized the world. More broadly, the conference institutionalized the idea of progress, which was confirmed by technological advances—telegraph, steam engine, railroad, clock, and so on. However, acceptance of this unified time occurred gradually: Japan unified time according to the twenty-four-hour clock in 1873 and synchronized that time to Greenwich mean time (GMT) on July 13, 1886; Germany unified time in 1893; France conformed to GMT in 1911; and the US did not officially accept GMT until March 19, 1918. Interestingly, the International Meridian Conference also codified the East and the West, the Orient and the Occident, by setting the beginning of the day at 180 degrees longitude, not at GMT. This unified time culminated the increasing synchronization of the world, the annihilation of time and space, and the rise of simultaneity in the twentieth century. These processes are, of course, highly uneven; Vanessa Ogle cautions that it was not until the 1950s that universal time became global (2015: 75–98).[28] Another way to characterize the spread of absolute time is in its relation to the rise of the nation-state and of industrial society. In short, our current use of chronological time is a metric that reinforces the liberal-capitalist system that emerged since the Enlightenment.

This is a good moment to bring up a statement by Serres, who describes the connection of progressive time to the global and technological history of nineteenth and twentieth centuries:

"Let me say a word on the idea of progress. We conceive of time as an irreversible line, whether interrupted or continuous, of acquisitions and inventions. We go from generalizations to discoveries, leaving behind us a trail of errors finally corrected—like a cloud of ink from a squid. 'Whew! We've finally arrived at the truth.' . . . That's not time, only a simple line. It's not even a line, but a trajectory of the race for first place—in school, in the Olympic Games, for the Nobel Prize. This isn't time, but a simple competition—once again, war" (Serres with Latour 1995: 48–49).

Serres's trenchant critique points to the way that linear time structures knowing and relations. Neither absolute time nor its application to society is neutral. The quantitative penchant (measurement) of chronology prioritizes competition—a race or even war. This is the history of the late nineteenth and twentieth centuries. It is perhaps a coincidence—but nevertheless an interesting one—that Eric Hobsbawm's *Age of Empire* began in 1875 around the same time that the world was synchronized according to absolute time and the historical discipline was becoming professional.

CLASSING OF TIME AND SPACE

This progressive time necessitates an obvious but unstated process, the "classing" (Serres 1995) or "breakup" of the whole (Lorenz and Bevernage 2013) into units that interact with each other.[29] Such classing is a constituent part of absolute time, necessary for the ordering and measuring of places, things, and events. It is the organization of parts into a whole—a competitive system.

This classing brings out the relation of absolute space and absolute time, and the repositioning of repetitive time in the application of absolute time to human society. In his discussion of the nation, Lefebvre argues that the nation arises from two moments, the market and violence.[30] The market is the place of repetitive activity that gives focus and hierarchy. Violence is the power that controls and exploits—in Serres's words, a race, competition, or war. The units that make up that "market" on the global level are the newly forming nation-states. I read Lefebvre as arguing that the nation-state is historical. It is spatialized time. Lefebvre writes, "According to Hegelianism, historical time gives birth to that space which the state occupies and rules over. . . . Time is thus solidified and fixed within the rationality immanent to space" (1991: 21).[31] In this repetition, time is spatialized; repetitive time facilitates a slowing down of time to formulate these units, the nation-state. My emphasis is on the interrelation between time and space, time-spaces (and the obfuscation created by absolute time and absolute space) in the classing or breaking up of time into subunits. I will discuss this relation between classing, nation-state, and history in the next chapter.

Repetition also slowed time in another way—presented as the opposite of linear time, repetitive time became identified as an originary temporality, closer to nature. It is a part of an early state from which forward motion emerges; it is akin to the repetitive worlds from which a modern society has developed. Things closest to an original state are removed from time. These are the past, dead, or inert objects. It enables what Carolyn Merchant calls the "death of nature": "The removal of animistic, organic assumptions about the cosmos constituted the death of nature—the most far-reaching effect of the Scientific Revolution. Because nature was now viewed as a system of dead, inert particles moved by external, rather than inherent forces, the mechanical framework itself could legitimate the manipulation of nature" ([1980] 1989: 193). Nature serves at least two functions. First, things within nature are inert objects to be used or exploited. Second, it serves as an origin from which, using chronological time as a metric, movement (i.e., development or progress) is measured. This is where repetition is inverted from a condition of stability to a condition of those on the lower end of this developmental scale: the primitive or backward people (labor) or societies (non-West) who are not quantifiably advanced.[32] Repetitive things that do not move forward are closer to a nature that embodies some state of lacking, and movement away from nature orders objects onto a scale of development. This connects well to the clockmaker who serves as the metaphor for man's (Merchant points out that this order is gendered) manipulation (i.e., improvement) of nature.

In the eighteenth century, this classing or spatialization was facilitated by a new technology that was gaining popularity—mathematics. Aggregates became a way to make sense of the heterogeneity of this expanding world.[33] Aggregation (and the numerical data such as averages) was a way to order the variation of individual cases. Serres, for example, writes, "A multiplicity marks and shows some redundancy, it becomes spatial when this repetition increases" (1995: 116). Through repetition or redundancy, commonalities, classings, categories, and places come into being. Like the allure of Big Data today, numbers and aggregates were a way to discern "secret patterns hidden inside masses" (Sheehan and Wahrman 2015: 60) so that they could be emplotted along a timeline to measure and compare. Individual variability is not eliminated but subsumed into some aggregate—categories of more or less like things. The heterogeneity of individuals gives way to the commonality of the category that is meaningful within a larger matrix. Bowker (2014: 572) calls this process of classing a "colonizing temporality." Probability provided a way to move the study of humans from individuals to categories; absolute time provided a way to measure and compare those categories. The result is the transformation of understanding from individuals and what they believe to quantifiable knowledge about people, things, and places.

Once the chronological order is classed, chronological time returns within each classed unit to naturalize, through history, that space.[34] The discovery of the past through chronological time and the emergence of mathematics and probability are deployed again, but this time it obscures the historicity of this new spatialized time. This form of successive time combines with a historical narrative that begins from some origin to the present day. This form of linking of events chronologically is Newton's duration, but this notion of duration is spatial.[35]

The mapping of categories (including nation-states) along the chronological structure, the use of chronology to write histories that naturalize those units, and the breakup of time into eras has provided a powerful sense of order for the international and now global world. We are able to map everything onto x and y coordinates of a time and space grid. This is what the great mathematician and philosopher Alfred North Whitehead calls "simple location." On the one hand, motion becomes stabilized as a mass (or event) that is between two points, while the mass has an existence independent of time. Whitehead describes this aspect of Newtonian time: "The material is fully itself in any sub-period however short. Thus the transition of time has nothing to do with the character of the material" (1925: 50). Everything has a distinct position in absolute space and occurs at unique moments that are measurable. This rendering of things according to simple location has been possible at a very reductive or simplistic level, but Whitehead disputes this very possibility: "I shall argue that among the primary elements of nature as apprehended in our immediate experience, there is no element whatever which possesses this character of simple location" (1925: 58).[36] I will take up this issue again in chapter 2; it is history that gives content to this simple location and makes it "real."

A fundamental problem with this system is the alignment of human action with the movement of matter. Henri Bergson points to the reductionism necessary to use this mechanistic reckoning for human consciousness. He writes, "We can understand that material objects, being exterior to one another and to ourselves, derive both exteriorities from the homogeneity of a medium which inserts intervals between them and sets off their outlines: but states of consciousness, even when successive, permeate one another, and in the simplest of them the whole soul can be reflected. We may therefore surmise that time, conceived under the form of a homogeneous medium, is some spurious concept, due to the trespassing of the idea of space upon the field of pure consciousness" ([1913] 2001: 98).[37] This application of Newtonian physics has been effective because of its simplicity (two variables), but we now know that when applied to people, systems, and ideas, there are many more variables.[38] We know that people and objects change as they move; they do not remain unchanged. Whitehead argues for what I will later call relationality, the "interconnectedness of things," both material and human. He appeals to an everyday experience rather than learned knowledge: "Your perception takes place where you are, and is entirely dependent on how your body is functioning. But this functioning of the body in one place, exhibits for your cognisance an aspect of the distant environment, fading away into the general knowledge that there are things beyond" (1925: 92). Historians might object that history covers this change of the unit. But in the adoption of Newtonian physics, an object, the nation-state, has been naturalized as a "mass" and removed from time before chronological time can measure its motion, duration, or rate. History structures the ordering of these masses, and it operates within the unit of the nation-state, the mass. I will discuss this separation of history into a system and the reinsertion of history of particular units in the next chapter.[39]

A temporal hierarchy emerges from the classings organized through this flow of time. There is a troubling connection to the emphasis on technology and its application to large units. This is one characterization of the history of the twentieth century—resource extraction, exploitation of labor, colonialism, and imperialism. But I will emphasize the implicit hierarchies of this system. On the one hand, we can cite Bacon's simple declaration that the recent is better than what existed before; indeed, the fetish of the new seems built into our thinking, but Serres writes rather caustically, "It follows that we are always right, for the simple, banal, and naive reason that we are living in the present moment" (Serres with Latour 1995: 48). But this is also part of a system that turns relational conditions into fixed temporal positions. One part of society that this system removes from history is what Lefebvre calls "lived time."

He writes, "With the advent of modernity time has vanished from social space. . . . Lived time loses its form and its social interest—with the exception, that is, of time spent working" (1991: 95). We see the effect of the escape from the clutches of time—the supremacy of space over time is the dominance of the state over lived experience, of the technological apparatus over the human.

In the context of this brief history of time, the relation between society and time is inverted. Time is now external to human activity, which is organized according to absolute time. Nowotny calls this focus an "intoxication with time" (1994: 26–32). This intoxication is in the freedom from the past, the order and predictability of the world, and speed—the perceived reduction of social and geographical distance. But this intoxication is possible by obscuring the role of chronology; it structures and orients. Michael Young speaks to this power within Nowotny's notion of intoxication: "By giving people a sense of control over their environment, technology has also encouraged them to think they can create their own future, and perhaps nothing has nourished linearity more than that" (Young 1988: 156). This intoxication is possible because the naturalization of absolute time along with its classing operations has removed this part of time, the historicity of time, from the historiographical operation. In his book *System*, Clifford Siskin notes the increasing connection between *system* and *history* by the end of the eighteenth century.[40] But it is not just adjacency but interrelation. He says that an unexpected finding is that *system* "shaped modern knowledge" by reshaping "history itself" (2016: 4). This system is the chronological structure—external time—that has ordered the world to become the framework in which modern history is written.

TWENTIETH-CENTURY TIMES AND CLASSICAL TIME

Interestingly, during the late nineteenth and early twentieth centuries, as absolute time was being used to organize knowledge about nation-states and academic disciplines emerged,[41] science was discovering that time is not mechanical and linear. Einstein's special theory of relativity demonstrates that the measurement of time is dependent on the framework of observation—that is, time is relative to the observer. "Relativity tells us there is no such thing as a fixed interval of time independent of the system to which it is referred" (Adam 2004: 61). Einstein calls this time *Eigenzeit*, often translated as "proper time."[42] This proposal of an *Eigenzeit* recalls the local notions of time of the medieval, non-West, and nonmodern places. It brings out the different times inherent to each unit of analysis. Moreover, the direction of time in a progressive system does not match the arrow of time in physics (Mitchell 2009: 43). The second law of thermodynamics is the only law of physics in which time is directional. However, that arrow moves toward dissipation and decay, not improvement and progress. Perhaps this dichotomy is one reason that thermodynamics has rarely been included in social applications of time. For my purpose, entropy requires that we recognize multiple outputs from the use of energy, even if it is not the desired outputs. Processes of development or progress also contain transformation that is closer to decay; in history, some of these outcomes have been marked as waste, ignorance, or unintended consequences.[43]

Again, as Adam (1990) points out, in the social sciences we have known for quite a while that studies often change the object being studied (quantum physics—the very acts of observation and measurement affect what is seen) and that perspective does depend on the position of the observer. Research in the humanities and social sciences also questions the notion of simple location and supports Whitehead's emphasis on relationality. For example, work on color perception shows that perceived color can change depending on adjacency (Albers [1963] 1975). Research in the cognitive and neurosciences shows that observation varies according to surrounding conditions and that environment does alter what is known and remembered (Vygotsky 1978; Hutchins 1995; Stafford 2007).

Research on reading and learning shows that people incorporate new information through their received understanding (Jauss 1982; Wolf 2008); complex systems theories offer a different way to think of connections, relations, and causality (J. Holland 1995; Mitchell 2009; Page 2008). In his discussion of the importance of entropy in social analyses, Fraser uses Escher's image "Ascending and Descending" to argue for the importance of the whole process and to place repetition and decay as central rather than an earlier, inferior, or external part of the process (1987: 281). This understanding of an internal time gains further support in cybernetics, the work of scientists seeking to connect the workings of machines to organisms during the second quarter of the twentieth century. What begins as an effort, in Jean-Pierre Dupuy's analysis, to "mechanize the human" ultimately exposes the limitations of classical time and points to the possibility of multiple times and the centrality of nonlinear temporalities.

A key element in this history of time is the recognition of biological times. At the turn of the century, biological work largely focused on collection, description, and classification. Darwin's evolution fits this classificatory tendency, and even though Darwin's evolution argues that adaptation leads toward greater diversity, its application to society by Herbert Spencer fits the ideology of progress according to a homogenous time. Two important mid-twentieth-century ideas that criticized linear science are the General System Theory (GST) founded by Ludwig von Bertalanffy and cybernetics, especially the work connected to the Macy Conferences (1946–53). Norbert Wiener describes cybernetics through a language analogous to history: "the study of messages as a means of controlling machines and society" (1950: 15). The messages (or, more commonly, information) of cybernetics can be likened to facts and data of history. We don't think of history as a mode of control, but it is a knowledge system that orders and guides. A key difference is that these sciences recognize the simplistic reductionism of classical science and offer more complex understandings and frameworks. Cybernetics and GST have often been merged as early attempts to overcome a key problem of classical science, the reduction of phenomena to two variables, or simple location (Pias 2016; Bertalanffy 1968). Warren Weaver, a key member of the Macy Conferences, calls the interests of classical physics "problems of simplicity" (1948: 536–37); Heinz von Foerster categorizes those problems as "trivial" (2014: 15–19); and Bertalanffy argues that it is the difference between a static (classical) and continuously changing (complex) system. We must remember that the basis of history, "simple location," is based on the classical physics they are criticizing.

One of the interesting connections of the Macy Conferences today is the belief that mechanical and physical laws, through what we now understand as digital technology, can be applied to biological processes. These scientists were ambitious; they sought "to design overarching orders of knowledge with nothing short of epoch-changing implications" (Pias 2016: 11). According to Dupuy, the goal was a "sciences of the mind" (2000: 77).[44] The initial title of the Macy Conferences, "Feedback Mechanisms and Circular Causal Systems in Biological and Social Systems," indicates the effort to bring together the biological and social through attention to nonlinear processes.[45] When the meetings began, Wiener suggested the analogy between organisms and machines. In 1955, Warren McCulloch still stated confidently, "Everything we learn of organisms leads us to conclude not merely that they are *analogous* to machines but that they *are* machines" (Dupuy 2000: 50). In Wiener's case, machines were technological (computational) objects; in McCulloch's case, they became "logico-mathematical being embodied in the matter of the organism" (Dupuy 2000: 50). It is hard to overstate the significance of cybernetics; it was a major development and warrants the assertion that this event marked the beginning of a second industrial revolution: first, the steam engine, and second, information theory based on digital forms.[46] It brought nonlinear time—circular causality, feedback loops, and homeostasis—to discussions of temporality. It helped spawn fields as diverse as information theory, computer science, artificial intelligence, autonomous systems, and cognitive science.[47]

Its limits, though, are in this ambition. In the records of the last five meetings, discussions also show the difficulty of applying the analogy of the machine to the mind. One of the pithy descriptors of cybernetics states that it is concerned with "ways of behaving," not the knowledge of things (Ashby 1956: 1). This focus on activity and doing when applied to biological and social systems necessarily encounters human variability. Some of the papers touched on perception—both psychological and physiological (through a frog's eyes)—language and symbolism, humor, emotions, and communication patterns in humans and animals. In a way, it replicates the separation of history. "Ways of behaving" emphasize the classifications, patterns of activity, and regularity of action in modern society. What is more difficult are issues that are beyond closed, classificatory problems such as the difference between causality and correlation, parsing abstractions, and performing logical inference (Jordan 2018; see also Marcus 2018). It should be an opening for scholars interested in processes by which humans know, decide, and act (like history).

A few did tackle these issues. Von Foerster founded his Biological Computer Lab, which gave rise to what has become known as second-order cybernetics. The key difference in second-order cybernetics is that the observer cannot be autonomous; the observer observes, is an actant, and reports. It questions the possibility of objectivity and points to the limitations of Newtonian science as "universal, deterministic, and objective" and with a neutral observer. This work punctuates the impossibility of escaping what Prigogine and Stengers call the "clutches of time" (1984: 213).

Finally, today, simultaneity is more apparent than ever. We have increasing writings, scholarly and popular, raising the compression of time to the extent that the future is frequently displaced by an extended present or presentism (Nowotny 1994; Hartog

2015; Harootunian 2015; Rushkoff 2013). As an example, Nowotny begins her book *Time*, "Today the tension between present experience that does not value what is past and an expectation oriented towards what is, in tendency, endless improvement has largely collapsed" (1994: 16). But rather than examining this changing relationality of time and space, today, in response to this collapse, we talk about innovation and invention as if they are different than improvement. Moreover, this seems to be our response to work that shows that the major technological discoveries that had the greatest impact on modern society occurred in the first half of the twentieth century (Gordon 2016). There is a conceptual disconnect. Society and academia seem so wedded to our chronological system—that is, have so naturalized its values—that the "new" suffices for innovation even though such improvements are usually a means of maintaining the past (the current structure), more efficiently. At minimum, we need to disaggregate processes. Michael Young (1988), for example, argues that we need to separate social evolution from progress—the existence of the former does not mean that there is progress. In his effort to revive the idea of progress, Peter Wagner separates social and political change from technological and economic progress. The past two centuries have seen the advance of the latter (enjoyed always by an elite), while the former is much more mixed. We still haven't addressed Simmel's sage observation: "The things that determine and surround our lives, such as tools, means of transport, the products of science, technology and art, are extremely refined. Yet individual culture, at least in the higher strata, has not progressed at all to the same extent; indeed, it has even frequently declined" ([1900] 1990: 448). In short, abstract time orders societies and fosters technological progress, and it is the latter that has, in Nowotny's words, intoxicated us to accept its elevation to a concept external to our world (1994: 26–28). In the rise of science, in the continued violence throughout the world, and in historical understanding, classical time is decreasingly apposite to our world (if it ever was).

To conclude this brief history, I return to the epigraph from Elias's essay on time where he calls for a "spring cleaning." We need to ask whether our application of absolute time to society has arrested our own development in the name of innovation and progress. Complex systems both close off history from the field and simultaneously provide an opening. The former occurs through emphasis on mechanistic forms of analysis; the latter appears in the limitations on addressing human variability. It provides fascinating possibilities for reconceiving relations between pasts and the present. Herbert Simon, more than fifty years ago, issued an oblique challenge to historians: "The profession of history places a greater value upon the validated particular fact than upon tendentious generalization. I shall not elaborate upon my fancy, therefore, but will leave it to historians to decide whether anything can be learned for the interpretation of history from an abstract theory of hierarchic complex systems" (1962: 473). This general avoidance of generalization in favor of the particular—the derision of theory at the start of this chapter—helps mask the role of history in maintaining what Postone (1993: 300) calls a dual temporality of modern capitalist societies underneath an ongoing, even accelerating flow; there is the conversion of time into a constant present—again, linear flow and repetition. In the next chapter I will explore how this dual temporality—motion and stasis—is enabled through the conflation of chronology and history.

CHAPTER TWO

HISTORY HAS A HISTORY

Newton's chronological writings might be called the mathematical principles of the consolidation of empires because they dealt primarily with quantities of geographic space in a temporal sequence; the individuals mentioned in his histories, usually royal personages, were merely signposts marking the progressive expansion of territories.... The subject matter of his history was the action of organized political land masses upon one another.

—Frank Manuel (1963: 137)

For three centuries maybe the objectification of the past has made of time the unreflected category of a discipline that never ceases to use it as an instrument of classification. In the epistemology that was born with the Enlightenment, the difference between the subject of knowledge and its object is the foundation of what separates the past from the present ... the "past" is the object from which a mode of production distinguishes itself in order to transform it.

—Michel de Certeau (1986: 216)

The history that showed things "as they really were" was the strongest narcotic of the century.

—Walter Benjamin (1999: 463)

In the introduction, I raised Kuhn's complaint that history obscures its research process. Kuhn's comment and Simon's observation at the end of the previous chapter (that historians focus on the particular) are connected in the merger between absolute time and history. Indeed, they operate together to obscure this historical process and naturalize each other—chronology and history. The combination serves as the basis for our understanding of the world, the overall structure of modern history (system), and the basic methods for historical inquiry (history). The "disguised" element of the historian's process is in the acceptance of chronological time as an external (i.e., absolute) time, the subsequent elision of this historical transformation, and the turn of history to the archives.

The success of this transformation is in, of course, the hundred plus years of the discipline. It also extends well beyond to historical thinking; Ermarth assesses the place of this historical thinking in the modern world: "Historical time, in fact, may be the most powerful value confirmed by the narratives of Western, especially Anglo-American, culture; it informs much of what we tell ourselves about individual and collective life. This convention underwrites the many touchstones of social, scientific, and economic thought in the West since the seventeenth century" (1992: 20). The power of historical thinking, and history as well, is in the way that it orders and orients us to certain ways of knowing about the past and our world.

This centrality of historical thinking contrasts the current worries in the discipline of history about a decline in interest and attention (and significance?) as well as a rise of a presentist mindset. Historians have generally blamed external factors, especially the denigration of humanistic understanding in favor of science and technology. While there is good reason for such a view, historians have ignored internal issues; we have so naturalized our processes that we have overlooked how history itself is a part of the problem. I agree with Ermarth (1992, 2011), who suggests that the history that developed over the twentieth century no longer matches changes to our societies conceptually, practically, or scientifically. This statement raises questions whether history too suffers from the fatal confusion Bastian (2012) identified in our understanding of time and nature. A naturalized chronological time is the foundation of this disconnect.

When the chronological structure is decentered, a richer, complex interaction between things before and anticipation becomes apparent. Things that happened often weigh heavily on anticipation as well as decision-making; they are not past and future but operations of evaluation, negotiation, and organization. Moreover, without the distance established by dates, we also begin to see commonalities between ideas, deeds, and sensibilities. For example, work in digital media suggests that communicating digitally bears more similarities with oral rather than written modes (Foley 2012; Saussy 2016). Work using "deep time" shifts subjects and perspectives where issues today might be similar to issues prior to the Enlightenment (Smail 2008, Standage 2013; Zielinski 2006). Augustine's notion of time might be closer to our lives in the twenty-first century: "It might be correct to say that there are three times, a present of past things, a present of present things, and a present of future things" (1961: 269). This seems to align better with Benjamin's quest for a history framed by *Jetztzeit*, an extended present. Benjamin's *Jetztzeit* was an attempt to extract humans from chronological time, not our current presentism as an extension of mechanical production. But if indeed we are in a world of an extended present, what does it mean for history and our understanding of the world (see, for example, Gumbrecht 2003; Hartog 2015; Nowotny 1994; Rushkoff 2013; White 2014)?

Certeau suggests that our current practice of history employs "bewitching voices of the narration [that] transform, reorient, and regulate the space of social relations" (1986: 207). The phrase "bewitching voices," like occlusion, points to a trickery or seduction in history itself, a similar effect to Benjamin's identification of "as they really are" as the narcotic of the twentieth century. Like magic, the trick involves distraction so that what is obscured has been hidden in plain sight, invoked frequently as a natural part of history. In this chapter, I argue that that bewitchment is made possible by the conflation of history and chronology. The obfuscation can be seen in manifold situations. For example, it is evident in the idea that developmental policies are applicable to different cultures at the same levels of development, irrespective of local circumstances and cultural differences. Or perhaps it is in the current fascination with algorithms that crunch masses of data, using the past (data) to instantiate and preserve the present in the name of (technological) innovation. This might lead to some kind of change, but often it is similar to the eighteenth-century application of mathematics to insurance (and chance) for profit. And today, we have new periodizations—Big History and the Anthropocene[1]— that attempt to deal with these changes. While both have some promise, they are within or subsumed by absolute time.[2]

From this brief introduction, I hope that it is clear that, by a history of history, I do not intend to write about how major figures—for example, Vico and Michelet—have written narratives and accounts of the past, beginning with Herodotus.[3] These operate in chronological time (even though chronological time did not exist) and reinforce—through a narrative of becoming—the naturalization of our current chronological structure of history. The historical structure that emerged during the eighteenth through twentieth centuries was a new way of conceiving and organizing social relations using the new technologies—linear, mechanical, and absolute time. Michel Foucault writes, "And it is in this classified time, in this squared and spatialized development, that the historians of the nineteenth century were to undertake the creation of a history that could at last be 'true'—in other words, liberated from Classical rationality, from its ordering and theodicy: a history restored to the irruptive violence of time" (1970: 132). This violence of time is the imposition of a new reality structured by a linear, mechanical chronology. By weaving itself into this time, history became the mediating system between science and society, a "squared and spatialized development." It created a world order; it changed the subject, object, data, and understanding of those it described (thereby colonizing them). History became a technology for order and control; it "transform[s], reorient[s], and regulate[s] the space of social relations" away from persons toward categories of people. In short, it changed what had been real to a new reality based on abstract, not experiential principles. It created a "virtual reality."

DISCOVERY OF THE PAST

People had (and have) different relations with and uses of pasts where what had happened is very much still a part of their present. To suggest that what has happened is gone and no longer part of the present is fantasy. One only has to look around, read (or listen to) the news, and think about how our lives are framed to recognize that pasts are constituent parts of our present. There are other ways of keeping previous happenings in the present. One form of recording was the annal, or the chronicle. Hayden White points to the following entries in the Annals of Saint Gall (1987: 6–7; blank years eliminated):

709. Hard winter. Duke Gottfried died.
710. Hard year and deficient in crops.
712. Flood everywhere.
714. Pippin, mayor of the palace, died.
718. Charles devastated the Saxon with great destruction.

As White points out, this is a list of extreme events that were a threat to "a culture hovering on the brink of dissolution" (1987: 7). Natural calamities and social events are not distinguished. Being, explanation, connections, causality, order of importance, and dates are not given. Yet White sees a thread: "Everywhere it is the forces of disorder, natural and human, the forces of violence and destruction, that occupy the forefront of attention. The account deals in qualities rather than agents, figuring forth a world in which things happen to people rather than one in which people do things" (1987: 10). The stable condition in nonmodern societies is not change but repetition, the continuation of the past—especially ideals of some exemplary founding figure (like Emperor Jinmu in the *Kojiki*[4]) in the present. Change did exist, but it occurred gradually through recurrence, was a devolution from the ideal beginning, and resulted from efforts to recover that originary state. Gurevich describes the aura of certainty in medieval Europe that existed in the repetitive present: "The past, as it were, returns continuously, and this lends solidity, gravity, a nontransient character to the present" (1985: 143).

Genealogy was another common mode of representing the previous happenings. This is closer to *historia magistra vitae*, exemplary deeds and figures, things, or happenings worth remembering to provide a sense of certainty when confronting a mystical and powerful cosmos. Gabrielle Spiegel points out that these forms often had political purpose—to authorize the present through connection to before—and were organized generationally, not chronologically (1997: 99–110). The subject was usually the individual or family line.[5] These examples suggest that nonmodern societies had a sense of before—a sense of its utility—and anticipation, but that is not the same as our understanding of the present between past and future. Moreover, the goal of the chronicler was transparency; he sought to convey faithfully what he heard or knew, including legend, unverified reports, and fables.

Newton himself shows the difficulty of the transition of history in his lesser cited *Chronology of Ancient Kingdoms Amended*. He did try to move history, especially the accounts of ancient kingdoms, into chronology. This is evident in the closeness of Manuel's description of *Chronology* to our international system, world, or global history. It can be read as ordering all onto one progressive timeline that quantifies—that is, measures and compares through interaction of now naturalized units—and it shifts the subject toward growth, hegemony, and violence. We can see how absolute time operates as the ahistorical structure for a historical narrative of a world order.[6] But emphasizing the connection to our current system is anachronistic and gets ahead of our story: *Chronology* shows the power of inherited forms of knowledge and that our application of absolute time to human activity was not that of Newton. Newton worked on *Chronology* for forty years, he frequently failed to precisely date events, and he predicted Armageddon in 2060 (Wilcox 1987: 208–14).[7] Nevertheless, he does move history closer to chronology.

Chronology uses an analogy that we still employ, the interchangeability between physical mass and human activity as aggregates or categories. Manuel's description of this work indicates two important changes: first, the subject of a chronological history becomes "quantities of geographic space in a temporal sequence" or "organized political land masses." It is the shift to place-based units, away from the deeds and thinking of individuals. History uses the demand for classing within universal time described in the previous chapter. Second is the presumption of motion; history describes the interaction, conflict, fusion, or destruction of these places. This is an extension of priority on the movement of mass in Newton's laws of motion to the expanded world. The relation between stability and change is now inverted.[8]

Our current understanding of history became possible with the differentiation of the past from the present (Certeau 1988: 2; Fasolt 2004: 12–22; and Schiffman 2011). The idea that the past had to be discovered is strange to us today. The key to this discovery was not a before but a past that is both prior and different (Schiffman 2011: 263). According to Zachary Schiffman in his careful study *The Birth of the Past*, Montesquieu was the first to use such a past in his efforts to write a universal history, *The Spirit of the Laws* (1748). Schiffman writes, "Montesquieu's writings represent a sea change in historical thinking . . . he showed how to deploy Cartesian analysis . . . using it to grasp the relations between distinctively human entities. In so doing, he distinguished between these entities by holding them at a remove from each other and measuring the distances between them" (2011: 209). Historians will no doubt disagree whether the emergence of a past can be located with such precision to one person. The eminent medieval historian Jacques Le Goff sees pasts emerging earlier and history evident from the sixteenth century. Nevertheless, it is clear that a new form of historical knowledge emerged with the Enlightenment and since the nineteenth century has developed into the basis of historical thinking today. Montesquieu's human entities are similar to "quantities of geographical space." Relations are understood through measurement of temporal distance. Interestingly, Montesquieu's *Spirit* is not chronological; his past facilitated comparison of political units and human sensibilities, but he did not do so sequentially (Toulmin and Goodfield 1965: 115–18).[9] A universal history did not necessarily mean a history according to chronological time.

Johann Gottfried Herder is another important figure who tried to merge history and absolute time. Like Montesquieu, his *History of Man* is not structured along a single timeline. Iggers calls Herder's historical structure "cosmopolitan culture-oriented nationalism" (1968: 30).[10] Herder echoes Newton in arguing that there are three primary concepts that serve as the organizing principles of the world of experience: time, space, and force (Norton 1991: 43–44, 141–43). He too accepted absolute time, the centrality of movement, and progress among human communities. Herder writes that reason "is not inborn in him; instead he attained it" (Zammito 2009: 79). But Herder's idea of history is not the historical structure we have accepted (Nisbet 1980: 270–72; Collingwood 1994: 88–93; Iggers 1968: 34–38). Herder dealt with this desire for a universal understanding of the myriad places of the world by arguing that peoples (races) have different characteristics and their development is conditioned by their internal conditions and environment.[11] On the one hand, he is trying to recognize the heterogeneity of peoples and of their development (or lack thereof). Yet in hindsight, his *History of Man* elevates the German people, and it would be a rather easy step to organize his history along a single timeline as does Hegel. But he did not take that step, instead criticizing universal history organized chronologically as Eurocentric (Iggers 1968: 35). This brings out one of those "differentials of time" that Benjamin sought. Herder recognized heterogeneity (still with hierarchies) but did not lock them into temporal categories.

Schiffman identifies Voltaire as the first historian to write a chronological narrative using a prior and distant past in his *Essai sur les moeurs et l'esprit des nations*. Georg Wilhelm Hegel, through his *Philosophy of History*, is, like Newton and his *Principia*, the intellectual most acknowledged for this transformation (here, of history). Hegel divided his world history into three successive conditions: the Original state (Oriental world) where repetition prevailed, the Reflective state (Greek and Roman worlds) of increasing self-consciousness, and finally the Philosophical state (Germanic world) where through Reason, one understands the Spirit. This structure of progress was taken to the nascent social sciences when Condorcet and Saint Simon sought to create positivism, which would turn history into a science of becoming. At this point, it is worthwhile to recall the breakup of time, what Serres calls "classing," as discussed in chapter 1. By the nineteenth century, absolute time also became linear historical time. The subject shifted to knowledge about organized political land masses, and nation-states were ordered according to their condition along a linear structure of development or progress. This brings out one of the central roles of a prior and distant past; the order it provided enabled comparison based on temporal measurement. Koselleck describes this process as the movement from a new time, *neue Zeit*, to modernity, *Neuzeit*. Modernity not only is an era but also "becomes a dynamic and historical force in its own right" (Koselleck 1985: 246).[12]

Interestingly, this convergence of chronology and history removes this *Neuzeit* from history; it becomes a system that orders the world. Siskin describes this relation between system and history: "With system now mediating the empirical connection to things—absolving history of that function—this was the moment in which temporality completed its move to history's core. New knowledge groupings now had empirical content arranged systematically *and* their own chronological narratives to define them and to differentiate them from each other" (2016: 56). The system that mediated the "empirical connections to things" is this absolute time applied to human society by the above intellectuals. It provides a structure of a whole but enables a turn away to the parts, which still are always emplotted onto the temporal grid. There is a shift from relational conditions to hierarchically structured temporal categories. For example, the Orient shifted from being an other of Greece, as in the work of Herodotus, to Montesquieu's static antithesis to a dynamic Europe, to the beginning of civilization in Voltaire, and to being the first stage of Hegel's world history and of Comte's positivism.

Ranke's claim to reality, *wie es eigentlich gewesen* (as it actually was), makes sense within this system. The chronological narratives that make up the parts parallel the chronological system. It continues to make sense in comparison with other claims because the structure within which he is operating is still our structure: absolute time. His famous line from his *Histories of the Latin and Germanic Nations* says, "To history has been given the function of judging the past, of instructing men for the profit of future years. The present attempt does not aspire to such a lofty undertaking. It merely wants to show how, essentially, things happened" (Ranke 1973: 137). Ranke is quite conscious of the transition of history from *historia magistra vitae* to a "scientific" history. Like Bacon's inversion, Ranke similarly inverts criteria from accounts that keep pasts in the present to knowledge about a past that stabilizes the present. This inversion stabilizes history in two ways. First, chronological history, in addition to absolute time, becomes an externality, a system. History, like time, becomes a metric for verifying, knowing, measuring, and comparing. It is with this idea that units move on a temporal and spatial grid that objectivity becomes possible.

Second, history maintains boundaries of the various spatial units, what Whitehead calls "simple location." The combination of this form of classing with history is, in my mind, one manifestation of what Whitehead identifies as the "fallacy of misplaced concreteness" (1925: 58). Simple location facilitates an emphasis on the idea that "things happened" as akin to matter ("organized land masses") and motion (their rise and fall). The focus on events in places turns history to the particular and away from the general. This operation is similar to a mapping process that Thomas Gieryn argues maintains the epistemic authority of science. Science, he argues, is not absolute but is defined through a cartography in which it is surrounded by "less believable or useful terrain" (1999: 4). Gieryn uses a "Map of a Great Country," where Mount Science is in the state of Great Knowledge and that state is between the states of Improvement and Fine Prospect and is near the state of Plenty and Enjoyment. As one goes farther away from Mount Science, on the other side of the Demarcation Mountains, one encounters the Territory of Indulgence and then Gloom, Poor Prospect, and Ruin (Gieryn 1999: 6–12). The map of the world, divided at the International Dateline, overlays onto the temporal division of organized land masses. Asia is to the east, Europe is at center, and the US is to the west; the Orient (primitive) is the East, and the Occident (advanced) is the West. In both cases, what Gieryn calls boundary work fixes relationality. In the case of history, this boundary work is maintained through a gesture of exclusion, the division of the old and new, or past and present. This gesture of exclusion will be described below.

The durability of this historical time suggests that it is (has been) seductive. History shifts from things worth remembering and keeping alive to knowledge that establishes order and prescribes measurable relations or truth. The problem is not that of objectivity or relativity; that dualism reinforces the basis of simple location. It returns us to Benjamin's statement in the epigraph that Ranke's notion of reality is the "strongest narcotic" of the twentieth century. It is an opiate for nation-states, those in power, as well as for the scholars who use it to claim relevance and importance. It has obscured the way that history transforms, reorients, and regulates.

PERFORMATIVITY OF HISTORY

It is important to acknowledge the brilliance of this historical time. First, it was key to the rise of the Enlightenment. Whitehead calls this transformation the "historical revolt"—the rise of historical thinking—simply "the study of the empirical facts of antecedents and consequences" (1925: 39). This notion of a revolt brings out the performative nature of the idea of history that we have taken for granted. It still structures, for better or worse, modern political, economic, and social systems; it has been very seductive. Moreover, this new history has been a key technology in addressing what Merchant, Siskin, Shapin, and others identify as the central concern of the era, the quest for certainty and order. Absolute time provided a structure rooted in science, and history provided a knowledge system to emplot all onto one progressive timeline that quantifies— that is, measures and compares through the interaction—growth, hegemony, and the violence of politico-cultural units. This is a part of the transformation and reorientation of what Certeau refers to as bewitching voices; the historical revolt was a shift to particulars. Each geographic space could write its own narrative within the structure of absolute time. For the nations, it offers the potential to write the "reality" of self and even correct what others think. History calls this inquiry into the development of masses within the structure "change over time" or "continuity and discontinuity."[13] In these phrases, history occludes its own history. This occlusion is in the removal of time from history as if it is, at the risk of perpetuating this misuse of Benjamin, "empty"; it is to ignore the politics of time. In the sections below, I will describe several ways that the performativity of history has been obscured.

Occlusion of Chronology

Chronology, of course, does not disappear; it is, though, delimited in ways that both make it obvious and neutral, as if without power to order and control. Even though the chronological structure of history is historical and is the very foundation of modern history, in the turn to the particular, time becomes both pervasive and limited; history is "transformed from within into a rational series of operations and objectified from without into a metric system of chronological units" (Certeau 1986: 216). The process Certeau describes can be attributed to two related moves: the separation of history from the philosophy of history and Ranke's emphasis on the veracity of documents and the turn to the archives.

A philosophy of history (as separate from history) also emerged with the application of history to absolute time. Voltaire was the first to employ the phrase "philosophy of history" (Collingwood 1994), and Hegel is well known for his *Philosophy of History*. In this phrase, Voltaire and Hegel open the possibility of separating this chronological system from histories within it. It serves as the overall structure of movement, then known as progress—a progression toward the spirit, from the Original to the Reflective and finally to the Philosophical state. We now shun these categories, yet the chronological structure still exists. This is where chronological time is, in Koselleck's words, "a dynamic and historical force in its own right" (1985: 246).[14] Chronological time simply is; there is no need for inquiry.

Once naturalized, history becomes a discipline that operates within that chronological system. Ranke is commonly cited as the iconic founding figure of modern history, especially the transformation of history to research on the particular, of nations using documents found in archives. He argued that the document is the best way to know events of the past, and the reconstruction of events from these documents results in an objective, real picture of the past. This is familiar, but Ranke relies on juxtaposition to support this assertion. In his essay "On the Relations of History and Philosophy," he separates the particular (history) from the abstract (philosophy) in order to argue for the veracity of archival research (Ranke 1973: 29–32, 33–46). An inversion occurs where the particular, though built on a now-hidden chronological system, is the part that leads to an understanding of the general and abstract. Siskin describes the connection of this history to a system with an occulted chronological structure: "This interaction [of parts to the whole] was the engine of Newtonian Enlightenment: *the calculus divided wholes into an infinite number of parts, and system connected parts into wholes*" (2016: 93). The parts are an acknowledgment of multiplicity, but because the general, the chronological system, is universal, difference is at best unevenness. This reliance on simple location allows for the illusion that history is like a jigsaw puzzle; the accumulations of parts (filling the gaps) leads to the whole (White 1978: 126ff). Ranke did not ignore the general; he identifies philosophy as the spirit or supreme idea of a society (echoes of Hegel; Iggers 1968); it transcends chronological time. But in doing so, he eliminates absolute time from philosophy and confirms that history operates in chronological time. (This is perhaps an early moment in the allergy of modern history to ideas, theory, and philosophy.) Time becomes a passing past-present-future that history operates within; the philosophy of history is timeless—it is about spirit and being. The chronological structure that orders the world is accepted as absolute. The politics of chronology, the way that time transforms, reorients, and regulates is, at best, backgrounded. Charles Hedrick, a historian of ancient Greece, writes, "With the development of an overarching chronographic system . . . history becomes 'one damn thing after another'" (2006: 50).

Particulars

The turn to the particular coincides with the process of "classing"; it is the combination of Newton's "organized political land masses" that fuse or destroy with Hegel's philosophy of history. This combination shifted the subject of history from human activity or quality of being to categories of humans, of the state and motion of those units. This shift from life to units was contested, for example, in the writings and appointment of Friedrich Wilhelm Joseph Schelling to the University of Berlin (Toews 2004: 1–7). John Toews describes Schelling's criticism of Hegelian philosophy as "whatness" (state or category) over "thatness" (quality or life): "Hegelian rationality shaped reality into a world of conceptual forms that defined experience but never penetrated beyond these forms to that prior ground of existence that made the shaping activity possible in the first place, and constantly threatened to break through the veil of concepts and reveal their contingent status" (2004: 5). This is another place where we can see how Certeau's bewitching voices "transform, reorient, and regulate." Toews's language is important: "rationality shaped reality" and conceptual forms "defined experience." Now the organization and understanding of life and experience is based on systems and categories, not human activity. History becomes a knowledge system (within chronological time) that values some collective singular, "quantities of geographic space in a temporal sequence" (Manuel 1963: 137). Previous happenings are transformed and reoriented into a past that describes some public, the collective singular.

Interestingly, despite its reliance on an absolute time that always flows regularly, this new history stops time—that is, the processes of life—by spatializing time. Newton's duration, what is between two points in time, allows for periodization—another spatialized time. We must recognize the work of scholars (like Bergson, Harvey, and Lefebvre) who have criticized this separation of absolute space and absolute time and instead argue that the two are always interrelated. Bergson unpacks the interconnectedness of time and space: "That time implies succession I do not deny. But that succession is first presented to our consciousness, like the distinction of a 'before' and 'after' set side by side, is what I cannot admit. . . . If we cut it up into distinct notes, into so many 'befores' and 'afters,' we are bringing spatial images into it and impregnating the succession with simultaneity: in space, and only in space, is there a clear-cut distinction of parts external to one another" (2002: 260–61). Drawing on Halbwachs, Hartog connects this spatialized time to a history that is an abstraction that, although borrowed, is separated from human activity. He writes, "History, which 'extracts changes from duration,' forges 'an artificial duration having no reality for the groups from which these events are borrowed'" (2015: 122). New units—places, taxonomies, and periods—are formulated by succession in chronological writing. This spatialization of time is the principal way that the classing gains historical form (Gross 1982: 59).

This inversion from quality to state is another moment when history turns to the particular, ensconced within but separated from the chronological system that structures history. It fills in the content for the classings that emerge from absolute time, making these newly formed spatializations appear as natural. Through succession and repetition, history marks temporal or geographic boundaries and provides a semblance of order amid motion. Absolute time, by definition, applies to numerous scales; it is deployed within these units as if it is addressing the "thatness." But this good faith effort to address quality is reoriented toward topics within that system—nations, identity, race, and class.[15] To recall Toews, this is a "world of conceptual forms" that don't penetrate to "that prior ground." From the nineteenth century, we see a proliferation of histories of nations. These are regulated by the temporal sequence, the chronological system that orders these units and serves as a metric of their differences, usually as the progress (or lack thereof) of the nation-state.

This turn to the particular—the nation-state—has been intox- icating. For Western nations, it provides a way to confirm their superiority in the world; for non-Western places, history (usually the lack of such) was invoked as evidence of inferiority, but it also became (and still is) a vehicle for critique, correction, and the hope for inclusion into the international order.[16] The twentieth century is strewn with efforts to move beyond the hierarchies and catego- ries of this system as well as to use them to rationalize imperial activities (e.g., Japan's Greater East Asia Co-Prosperity Sphere, what we can call an alternate modernity). A question that will be addressed below is to what extent this future is captive of the past; the past as "prior and different" by definition always validates the West as the new, the future, or of the future as a continuation of some teleological process that can only move forward along a continuum from the past.[17]

Gesture of Exclusion

Perhaps the most devious way that history obscures its performa- tivity is within the linear structure itself. On the one hand, the bewitching operation is in the ordering, the hierarchical metric toward an ideal end. Work on the history of time and of history has tended to focus on the linearity or progressive nature of this time. That is its main ostensible structure. I also followed this path. Yet as I discussed in chapter 1, linear time operates with cyclical processes, and increasingly scholars are again recognizing that this linearity depends on other forms of time and displaces these times in ways that support this linear structure (Michael Young 1988; Sharma 2014; Irani 2019; Koselleck 2018). Certeau calls this operation a "gesture of exclusion" (discussed below), Serres calls it a "dogmatic expulsion," and Marx calls it "formal subsumption."[18] These operations demonstrate the way that pasts in the language of succession are transformed, reoriented, and regulated to main- tain constantly the superiority of the modern. This is a temporal

form of the boundary work Gieryn uses to describe the maintenance of the authority of science. While there is a structure and
ostensible possibility for progress or improvement using Newtonian duration, the boundary between past and present, or old
and new, is a relational condition that does not lead to changing
relations because the latter is defined by juxtaposition against the
former. In the perpetual movement to some new (modern, Occident), an old (tradition, Orient) continually reinforces that new.
The gesture reinforces those identified as modern and locks those
identified as past into a repetitive condition—always the "not yet"
(Chakrabarty 2000: 6–11). To repeat Serres, "it follows that we are
always right, for the simple, banal, and naive reason that we
are living in the present moment" (1995: 48). This is the success
and limitation of the historical revolt—it grounds thinking that is
freed from the authority of a past but locks those described as past
into a constant condition of incompleteness. Elizabeth Povinelli,
drawing from Chakrabarty, visualizes this condition as the "imaginary waiting room of history" (2002: 77).[19]

This is one of those areas where the performativity of history is
disguised (hidden) in the very process that enables it. The past, now
naturalized simply as previous moments in chronological time (the
"old"), plays a critical role in affirming the "new," the modern, and
the most advanced. Certeau describes this "gesture of exclusion" in
his study of mystics in sixteenth- and seventeenth-century France.
This gesture employs some past or marginalized object as one
side of a binary from which a society distinguishes itself (Certeau
1992: 17). Though his discussion focuses on heretics, he is clear
that this position of other as past has been employed using many
other groupings of marginalized people; he mentions cultural and
ethnic minorities, spiritual marginalities, the Indian, the mad, the
child, and the non-West (1988: 3; 1992: 18). Peoples now classified
as some past facilitate the process of classing, of making nations.
They give definition to boundaries that show progress—not as
much by internal conditions as by juxtaposition that is focused

on state, not quality.[20] Marx identified this process over a century ago as formal subsumption, a process by which the past is incorporated, used, abstracted, and reassigned, not replaced. Harootunian writes, "Surviving practices from prior modes of production were not 'remnants,' as such, but rather appeared as historical temporal forms no longer bound to the moment and context in which they had originated, now acting in a different historical environment serving the pursuit of surplus value" (2015: 11). In this gesture of exclusion, repetition is inverted from a stable condition of societies to a form that stabilizes both linear history itself and the condition of being modern. People of difference are transformed into some characterization of repetition; they are closer to nature, the origin, or primitive. They are regulated through the repetition of the gesture itself. Repetition is in the constant monitoring of historiographical boundaries (pasts), but the operation occurs through the structure rather than the conscious acts of the historian. For example, dating calls for the comparison of things across time; it reinforces the new as juxtaposed to the old. This history is not the particular accounts of individuals but the maintenance of the historical structure that is a temporal hierarchy. For the modern, the "same" is a process by which it is forever "new" and a "historical *form*" more than a homogeneous (or unified) *content*. I should emphasize that this position of the excluded is not necessarily meant to be derisive. Kathleen Davis points to the dual character of this position—the revered or respected origin in contrast to a strange/different other (2010: 59).

The two levels of history, as system and as particularity, ensure the perpetuation of that "imaginary waiting room." As long as chronology remains, this gesture of exclusion is a constituent part of history. Fasolt has complained, "So long as there is history, there must be a Middle Ages," and he acknowledges the many but ultimately futile "well-intentioned efforts" to extract oneself from this position as a modern other (2004: 228). We can just as easily replace medieval with Asia (Orient) or some other non-Western place.[21] Some past other (temporal or geographical) preserves and reinforces the privileged position of the modern in history. A predicament of historians of medieval and early modern Europe and of non-Western places is that the structured categorization of these periods or places is built into historical chronology; they are some version of incompletion or a primitive form of the modern (Spiegel 1997; Gurevich 1985; Fasolt 2004; Cole and Smith 2010; Chatterjee 1986; Chakrabarty 2000; Harootunian 2007). The boundary work constantly performed by the past is hidden in the argument for linear movement and ensures the stability of the system itself.

Tombs of Data

Up to this point, I have argued that the performativity of history is in its chronological system. I have discussed the connection to the change of subject, a transformation of "reality," and the inversion of repetition that accompanies and maintains the linear structure of history. A reason for the longevity of this system is its scalability. As Siskin (2016) points out, the relation between whole and parts or between system and history also operates within each part—the nation-state to the human. Now, I turn to a smaller fundamental unit of history, the document and the "fact," where performativity reaches the research practices, the ongoing filtering system of historians. It is perhaps the activity where the "violence of time" is most obscured. Certeau describes the violence of this act as a form of pacification: "This project aims at 'understanding' and, through 'meaning,' at hiding the alterity of this foreigner; or, in what amounts to the same thing, it aims at calming the dead who still haunt the present, and at offering them scriptural tombs" (1988: 2). The focus on document as the basic unit of historical evidence is a form of control, "scriptural tombs" (or archives), both to limit the multiple possibilities within a document and to constrict recorded happenings to only particular parts of the past.

To a large extent, I have told a story of becoming, the merger of chronology and history. This connection, however, was not obvious. It took almost a century to merge chronology and history into the history we practice today (Wilcox 1987: 187–220). For example, despite his contribution that brings chronology closer to absolute time, history for Petavius was still an account of human activity—acts, thoughts, meaning, and arguments—in which time is internal. He writes, "History has as its own to possess fully the matter of deeds and to write down their order, usually with proofs, arguments, and witnesses, whence the order of individual years is established. Chronology indeed inquires after one thing, by what signs and marks each thing may be arranged in its years and times" (quoted in Wilcox 1987: 205). The difference between the systems he was trying to merge can be illustrated through Herodotus. Herodotus synchronized the chronologies of Athens and Persia around the invasion of Athens as follows: "Kalliades was the archon in Athens in the sixth year after the death of Darius, when Xerxes went to Greece" (Momigliano 1990: 38). We know this year is 480 BC.

The contrast between the locally specific information of the former against the abstractness of a year is stark. The translation of event markers into years transforms understanding.[22] Dates were not noteworthy in many societies. For example, even though 776 BC is the commonly accepted date of the first Olympic Games, that year was not recorded (historians disagree about the year they actually began), and instead, the games themselves marked time. It is the same for the birth of Christ; it was not on December 25, and we now know that the calculation of years is probably four years off (Dionysus Exiguus is the source of the error). These different sensibilities are also evident in the founding of the Hattori Watch Company (Seiko)—an icon for what became the temporal precision of Japan—it varies. In the US, the celebration of birthdays on the date of birth began in the late nineteenth century, a custom that emerged from Hallmark Cards' search for a new market (Chudacoff 1989).

These are examples of the ways that dating has given meaning to past events through modern criteria, not through the contemporary sensibilities. Petavius did create three rules for the application of dates to history so that they could be ordered according to a single time. First, he identified a date based on authority (corroborating evidence based on reliable accounts). Second, he abstracted the date based on demonstration (astronomical evidence). Third, he used hypothesis (convention; Wilcox 1987: 206–7). The first two rules are close to our current practice, but in the inclusion of convention, Petavius was still allowing traces of the past, especially of exemplary figures and deeds where meaning was situated within a range of interactions.

This turn to documents or "facts" is generally attributed to Ranke, beginning with his research on Venice in the 1830s. Ranke argued that documents (primarily of diplomats and civil servants) offered the material closest to the past and an objective view (Eskildsen 2008). Historians have shown that Ranke's faith in the veracity of documents was optimistic, but I am less concerned with objectivity than the transformation of accounts into data.[23] Like Petavius and historians before him, Ranke sought to determine which information to use. Wolfgang Ernst calls this transformation of material into facts a process of desemiosis (2002). Nowotny's description of the scientific method as cleansing is apt; it is a process of identifying, naming, classifying, and discarding.[24] Ranke compared documents to other sources and especially used names and dates for corroboration and veracity. He "pointed to disagreements and inconsistencies among texts to determine their historical value" (Eskildsen 2008: 436). In Meiji Japan, Kume Kunitake and Shigeno Yasutsugu used similar methods to cull through texts in their project to collect documents, archive them, and write a history of Japan. Cleansing occurred; errors in dates, even though chronological time might not have been a critical marking mechanism, and even misspelling of names were enough to disqualify the authenticity of some documents.

This methodology altered the import of written traces that had served as authoritative sources for knowledge about earlier events. Those that could not measure up to these new criteria have become quaint or primitive stories—important because of their originary status, yet denigrated as historical evidence (these become national literature).[25]

This brings out the "return" of chronological time, or what Ernst calls a process of resemiosis. Dating facilitates the shifting of pasts from something living in people—meaning and values—to a dead past—empirically verified facts. Now chronological time enables a precise mapping of events and data, independent of individuals, place, or the matrix of relations from which they emerged. This is a part of that virtual reality, "mathematic principles of the consolidation of empires"—again, "simple location." The place of their creation is replaced by a classing system, often the nation and its institutions. As Certeau points out, the "real" as represented by historiography does not correspond to the "real" that determines its production. In this case, dates organized chronologically are applied to order the particulars of history, the subunits—mass, classing, geographical space, or especially the nation-state. But it is important to heed Harold Innis's work that shows the bias of media in societies and civilizations (1951). Documents are biased toward a few leaders, institutions, and fixity. This focus contracts pasts into a reduced realm that is acceptable for historical inquiry. Historical data are shorn of a vast array of evidence about pasts. Stories give way to information; they are further fragmented into "facts" disembodied from their place of former significance (Benjamin 1968a). Data become portable; they become a commodity. What historians call context is not the situatedness but the specific time and location of events. This move further separates what becomes this chronological system (world progress) from history (the writing of the becoming of a people—particular). More important, it provides a way to give the Newtonian "mass" a simulacra of qualitative change.

The qualitative element of that history is limited. Ranke (and historians) argued that the particular fits in the general but without interrogating this general.[26] Indeed, history today has a hard time integrating the domestic with the international even though both reinforce each other. Efforts to move beyond this limitation have tried to move away from the national yet do this through the national—during my career, we have tried new nominal forms for (but never replaced) international such as area studies, postnational, multinational, transnational, and global. While I still have hope for the global, nation-states still serve as the principal units of analysis, and the structure of West and the rest prevails. More important, the chronological metric orients history toward technological development and the political and economic deeds of the nation-state; emphasis is on quantitative measurement and comparison.

This history was a part of a larger pattern of "science," which formulates knowledge systems that order the world. Carolus Linnaeus ordered living organisms into genus and species. Anthropology emerged at the end of the nineteenth century to know those outside the West (see, for example, Fabian 1983; Pratt 1992; Raj 2007; and Richards 1993). Statistics, which began in the previous century, was accepted into the British Association for the Advancement of Science in 1833.[27] In each case, data became important as a way to mark its place in some category beyond its immediate environment or the moment of creation.

The identification and collection of documents, the extraction of data from stories, is coterminous with the rise of national archives. There is a clear connection of the rise of the modern archives to the nation-state. The *Archives nationales* was founded following the French Revolution, and the British Public Records Office was founded in 1838.[28] Ranke increased attention to archives after 1830 when he was disturbed by the revolutionary activity surrounding him. When he began, documents were scattered; research was more akin to field work. The organization of documents into official archives gives this new reality—a "virtual reality"—material structure: pieces of paper—records—organized according state categories and to scientific standards—chronology. The key organizing principles (*respect des fonds*, or provenance) support this change in subject away from humans toward institutions (Eastwood 2010). Ranke's turn to the archive brought his history and affinity for the state closer to the goals of the state.

It strikes me that this structure and institutionalization is another fatal confusion in which history has become overly focused on itself. There is a rising interest in the past but a decline in interest in academic history (de Groot 2009). History has ceded a huge swath of the past—human sensibilities and beliefs for this appeal to documents. This focus has also restricted the range of the past—artifacts and ruins are the domain of archaeology (Holtorf 1996), paleography covers humans prior to settlement (Smail 2008), and literature focuses on human sensibilities and emotions. Environment, inherited structures, received knowledge, belief, and experience all affect reception, interpretation, and meaning.

It is important to reconsider our notion of the document and the "fact." The work of intellectuals prior to and during the Enlightenment bears suggestive commonalities with recent arguments by scientists and the work of psychologists and cognitive scientists that demonstrate the specificity of the event as interconnected. They suggest that our current thinking might be the anomaly, not the norm.[29] I will discuss these sciences in the following chapters. I will remain suggestive, invoking a philosopher and a historian: Whitehead's "interconnectedness of things" and Certeau's notion of a text or document as a "theatre organized by the vocabulary and syntax of a moment of history" (Certeau 2015: 22). For these scholars, sources or "facts," are not objects that exist, isolated from the milieu of their becoming; they have undergone a "cleansing." Instead, when documents are considered as nodes of activity, they occur among different actors with varying inscriptions and differing forms. The "fact" is not always the same. The understanding during the moment of eruption, the language of bodies, the places of writing, and of course, the moment of interaction possibly alter its meaning.

Second-order cybernetics is especially relevant here for recognizing the roles of inherited knowledge and the observer. We must also be aware that the document is also information that embeds historical knowledge and that actors use to make their decisions. Multiple perspectives exist; the observer observes, records, and participates; this process is repeated by historians. As information, the document too has a history and has been received differentially. This understanding of a document as a node corresponds to struggles to understand the significance of the past in the sixteenth century (Grafton 1994). Historians might counter that we do this through context. But again, there is an inversion. Context reinserts surroundings after documents are extracted from their situatedness. In the following chapters, I argue that historians must return (or move toward) this notion of the situatedness of data and of information. It is increasingly important in today's societies that are forsaking pasts for the present.

HISTORY AS MYTH

The institutionalization of this understanding of history occurred at the end of the nineteenth and early twentieth centuries. Interestingly, this is almost simultaneous to the relegation of absolute time to classical time. The chronological structure of history, the basis of what we call historical thinking, is at best one form of time that remains, primarily because of its deep legacy. Yet we persist on using it as if it were absolute. Efforts throughout the twentieth century to suggest other temporal structures have not had much success. Perhaps today is different; this is also the period when communication and knowing are shifting from print to digital, the second period of information inflation. We are only now beginning to deal with this transformation.

In the introduction, I invoked Serres, Blumenberg, and Mali to suggest that the acceptance of the merger of chronology and history maintains this mythical mode (our current system). It is a conceptual system that is linear and regular, homogenizes life according to mechanical, linear processes, and encompasses variation as unevenness (with an enticement that one can become equal). In its merger with history, chronological time has become a social technology that guides and controls us (Mumford 1964). It imposes structure, an ordered mechanical life; it values measurables, especially technology and economics; it relegates humanistic work—ideas, culture, interpretation, and ethics—to a secondary or lesser value compared to measured work; and it guiles us into thinking that we are better than before.

We must admit, though, that this myth is seductive. The seduction of this history is in a hidden boundary marking and maintenance system that enables us to identify the problems of others and thereby create for ourselves a progressive position, which amounts to what Fasolt calls "well-intentioned efforts" (2004: 228). The gesture of exclusion operates among historians and within historical thinking—because we are more recent, we know more than "them." Those of the past give us certitude that we are more advanced, that we are correct; because they are before or behind, they are marginal and not yet informed—or worse, we will "help them." Perhaps that is why Benjamin identifies "as they really were" as the strongest narcotic of the twentieth century. History is a core discipline of the social sciences and humanities; it ostensibly explains and constitutes our political and economic systems; it orders the globe; and it confirms our professional identities— "as a historian."

That certitude, however, depends on the occultation of the performativity of chronological time that takes a relational condition and elides that relationality by assigning temporal positions within a system believed to be natural. Ranke has bequeathed us a history that, in the name of objectivity, allows for the transformation of cultural difference and conflict "into conditions for a progressive political and ethical struggle for unity and reconciliation" (Toews 2004: 373). That has not worked; the globe is too heterogeneous to formulate a unified order, especially one that is hierarchical. We must explore other ways to think about the significance of pasts in our present. There are hints in the past (prior to the Enlightenment); there are new understandings in the sciences that we must consider. I would argue that it is even more important in our digital age than ever.

INTERLUDE

But . . . if I were asked to help make the people of the world receptive to the demands of a time-compact order, I would first try to make history appear irrelevant. It is much easier to secure cooperation among people without an understanding of history than those with many and usually antagonistic histories.

—J. T. Fraser (1987: 314)

A civilization which cannot burst through its current abstractions is doomed to sterility after a very limited period of progress.

—Alfred North Whitehead (1925: 59)

The epigraphs from Fraser and Whitehead speak to the emergence of a historical thinking that operates today. I connect our current worries about the place of history and the humanities to Fraser's worry that history appears irrelevant. History is the chronological structure that has naturalized our understanding of the world according to a linear, homogenizing time—Fraser's time-compact order. This irrelevance is a logical progression of the discipline from abstract criteria that separate human experience from historical reality. Fraser's nightmare of compliance brings to mind the novels of Aldous Huxley and George Orwell. Yet it also speaks to scholarly work, such as that of Gumbrecht, Hartog, G. H. Mead, Nowotny, Runia, and others who bring up the increasing presentism that characterizes the twenty-first century. We increasingly live in a world where we are locked in the perpetual present of the time-concept order. Massimiliano Tomba echoes Whitehead in the following rather graphic statement: "With the early image of the Robinsonades, the hostile behaviours of individual atoms were hurled into a meta-historical state of nature, thus creating a logical-historical circularity capable of immobilising transformation and producing the elements of economic and political modernity: individuals. This image has acted beyond all expectations, bringing about the complete animalisation of the human who lives in a world without history" (2013: 61). Today, we seem to be locked into this world of immobilized transformation. In the name of innovation, search engines use data from pasts to generate and fulfill human desires, while technological "advances" seem to improve what we have; both further lock us into a future perfect.

The more I have worked on time in modern society, the more I feel as if I am writing about a history of what has been forgotten in our craft of history. One can interpret Fraser's warning as a danger for society with a poor sense of history. Few historians would disagree. But I would suggest that the problem is within history itself; we seem to be caught within a loop of our own making. History is built on a structure that abstracts our work (despite usually "well-intentioned efforts") from human activity, even though the discipline claims to speak about and for the human. Yet this poor sense of history can also emerge from a history abstracted from human experience. Historians (and humanists) have had the luxury of juxtaposing our work against the sciences and technologically oriented fields; thus we believe that we speak for the human and the humanities—or so we argue. This too is an example of the boundary work, the operation of the gesture of exclusion. Just as the break from the past (the before) authorizes the new (the same), history uses this gesture to maintain the fiction that it too is not a technology but an advocate for the past (human) against the new (technology).[1] Yet I hope that the previous chapters have shown that the merger of chronological time and history has created a technology that has masked the mechanical conceptual framework of our world. The danger of this acceptance can be illustrated by Hans Saussy's observation on writing as a technology: "The more pervasive a technology, the more it is apt to become invisible, to take charge of the thinking of those seeking to think about it and school them in the selectiveness of its perceptions" (2016: 63). Self-reflection is insufficient.

History has a rich literature of protestations that we are critical and reflexive. Chris Lorenz (2014: 57) has an apt analogy. It is as if historians can will away the 130-year coal fire in Xinjiang province (that will require 30 years of cooling) by exhorting, "Fire, go out! Just go away!" Often, we invoke important historians to critique a part of history only to discover that the critique reaffirms the overall historical structure. Marx, Benjamin, and Braudel are three examples; they are recognized, often respected. Yet the discipline has rendered their work into segments that support the linear narrative rather than to using their ideas to increase the complexity and significance of many histories that are evident. We end up with exasperated comments that lament that chronological, objectivistic history is still the norm. More recently, the forum in the *American Historical Review* (Akyeampong et al. 2015) on change provided a good example of this resiliency. Excellent historians, together in a state-of-the-field discussion, concluded with the standard—continuity and discontinuity, an idea that assumes and supports the status quo.[2]

To move beyond this circularity, it is important to remind us of Certeau's inversion: "To 'historicize' our research in placing it back into a contemporary configuration on which it is dependent, and to 'dehistoricize' *mystics* in showing that one cannot reduce it to a past positivity" (2015: 9). This is a recognition of the ways that our current history, though historical and performative, has been accepted as natural and objective. An example of this process of inversion is Richard White's *Remembering Ahanagran*, a fascinating account of his family's past in twentieth-century Northern Ireland.[3] Superficially, it is an account of White's journey into his family's past. Yet it is also a story of the different pasts that exist—White's, his family's, the community's, and Northern Ireland's, Ireland's, and England's:

> I [White] did not understand the Troubles, I didn't understand Kerry, and I didn't understand how time worked in Ballylongford . . .
>
> When I try to fit these stories into a history, I encounter pasts that do not speak the same language. They do not follow the same rules. . . .
>
> But in Sara's stories the past is not a single frame. There are different pasts that hang like two pictures on a wall. One frame is the everyday. Within it everyday acts are repeated endlessly. And when acts are repeated, there is no need to specify the time of each act or indeed, the separateness of each act, or who, exactly, performed it. . . .
>
> The everyday does not include the extraordinary. To account for the extraordinary, Sara and Kerry have another way of remembering: the Times of Troubles. . . .
>
> What history keeps distinct, this common memory of the Troubles joins together. . . . The monks died in 1580. Eddie Carmody died in 1920. . . . The frame of the Troubles is to understand the dying differently. There are not multiple deaths in the Troubles, there is but one death endlessly repeated. It is a heroic death, and it cries for vengeance (1998: 35–37).

This passage illustrates Certeau's inversion, that we historicize our research and dehistoricize our objects of research. The issues I address in the following chapters are evident in this passage. We see the gesture of exclusion at work: for history as chronology, White's description can be static society, a story of the repetition of daily life of his Ireland. Moreover, the repetition of the deaths in 1580, 1920, and so on proves the backwardness (a lack of historical understanding) of the inhabitants and the need for power (British imperial) to maintain the order—that is, the unevenness or hierarchy of the imperium over the colony. But on the other hand, we see the possibility of understanding pasts without that gesture of exclusion. White's account does not flatten lives into a chronology based on dates; he struggles at first but ultimately does not force others into his chronological time. Instead, he describes some of the understandings and uses of pasts that highlight how people act and relate, the process of living. Their time is configured according to their lives and events; time is internal. The constancy of daily life and the recurrence of the extraordinary demonstrate entropic processes—death and decay exist—as well as the modes of maintenance that often lead to change. The Troubles show a different understanding of duration—not as successive events between two dates but as a moment when past and present are the same. It is not that the inhabitants don't understand that things happened, but what is remembered is not distant (a dead past) but still a part of the present. The value here is in family and community. But we also see different times that are layered: the time of history (i.e., the British imperium), the juxtaposition of migrants to the US and their return home, the Troubles, and the everyday. There are points of conjunction, and often they remain separate. Perhaps this is how life operates.

The following chapters will take up these issues, which question the normative units of the historical tool kit, the "fact," the nation-state as unit of analysis, the emphasis on material and measurable things, and notions of change. I hope that the next chapters, at the very least, unmask the masquerade of chronological history and open the possibility to expand the ways that scholars approach pasts, from knowledge of the past to understanding of previous happenings as relational; it is guided by human activity rather than abstract categories.

CHAPTER THREE

HETEROGENEOUS PASTS

The supposed unity of time projected by capital and nation-state is a masquerade that invariably fails to conceal the ceaseless confrontation of different times.

—Harry Harootunian (2015: 23)

Variety and possibility are inherent in the human sensorium—and are indeed the key to man's most noble flights—because variety and possibility belong to the very structure of the human organism.

—Norbert Wiener (1950: 52)

The most fundamental feature of history is not the unity, uniformity, and homogeneity of Newtonian or Hegelian time, but indeed the plurality, multiplicity, and heterogeneity of socially and historically conditioned temporalities.

—Helge Jordheim (2014: 505)

The epigraphs above from Wiener and Jordheim emphasize that heterogeneity is inherent to life—biologically and conceptually—but, as Harootunian points out, for centuries we have accepted a myth or masquerade that has (imperfectly) hidden this essence for a fictive unity, a unity rooted in chronological time. My goal of this chapter is to explore the possibility of heterogeneity serving as the basis for historical inquiry where difference does not become an unintended outcome, a good that serves as ornamentation, or a place/idea/person needing correction.

The difficulty of any discussion on the heterogeneity of time is the inclusion of difference within absolute time. Different times are hidden in plain sight as the unevenness that makes up linear time. I differentiate this form of variation as unevenness rather than heterogeneity.[1] The ubiquity of absolute time throughout our knowledge system makes confusion easy. The increasingly common phrase "multiple temporalities" is often a part, not a critique, of absolute time. Althusser and Balibar describe the problem: "We should indeed be relapsing into the ideology of a homogeneous-continuous/self-contemporaneous time if we related the different temporalities I have just discussed to this single, identical time, as so many discontinuities in its continuity; these temporalities would then be thought as the backwardnesses, forwardnesses, survivals or unevennesses of development that can be assigned to this time" (1970: 106). Critique—discontinuities in its continuity—remains beholden to absolute time and the Hegelian system. This conflation of difference into unevenness is a part of the masquerade; it compounds the difficulty of discussing and rendering understandable times where absolute time is not the standard.

My effort to formulate an understanding of pasts through a different epistemology of time is to turn to recent science, the "new," and to pasts, the "old." Much of what I call the "new" has been around for more than one hundred years. It is from the physics of special relativity, thermodynamics, quantum time, and now complex systems; it is also from the greater understanding of biological processes that became common in the mid-twentieth century. It would be a contradiction in an essay that argues for heterogeneity to call for the replacement of these "new" concepts over the old, classical time. That would invoke the gesture of exclusion. It is possible for these times to coexist. Like our use of Newtonian time, there is not a direct application or transfer of physical or biological times to social forms. My hope, though, is that we see that the disciplines are not as distinct as our practices suggest and that the adaptation of this "new" can help us extend historical thinking into the twentieth century. Scholars such as William Connolly, Barbara Stafford, and Helga Nowotny have already shown the potential ideas from the neurosciences or physical sciences for broadening our understanding of the humanities; history can too. The disguise or masquerade is being exposed.

This is also an opportunity to revisit the "old," but I run the risk of invoking the ancient/modern dichotomy or a "golden age." So be it, but without a chronological metric, the "old" and "new" can suggest an isomorphism rather than difference where neither the new nor the old is better. For example, Bertalanffy locates the origins of General System Theory in the ideas of Nicholas de Cusa, a sixteenth-century mystic. Bertalanffy rightly points to de Cusa's notion of "learned ignorance," the impossibility of knowing the absolute truth, and "coincidence of opposites," or that every reality is manifold and depends on perspective (Bertalanffy 1968: 11, 248; Certeau 2015: 23–70). Increasingly, scholars are recognizing the ways that pre-Enlightenment figures sought to deal with information inflation, the decline of the church, the expanding world and its many locals, and the quest for some universalism. Fasolt shows the situatedness of Hermann Conring's texts, and Jordheim points out the more sophisticated understanding of times among eighteenth-century historians, such as Johan Christoph Gatterer (Fasolt 2004; Jordheim 2017). To argue for relational notions of space-time, David Harvey draws on Leibnitz, who criticized Newton's absolute time and space and argued that time has no independent existence (Harvey 1996: 250–64; see also Hölscher 1997). Interestingly, the ideas of such "old" early modern scholars compare well with recent scholarship, including on chronobiology and digital media. The old and new sandwich absolute time.

Perhaps it is absolute time and our understanding built on it that is the anomaly.

I have increasingly wondered why histories of human activity follow a mechanistic, physical time to understand organisms and organic processes.[2] The use of biological times rather than classical time to order history was also a possibility in the late eighteenth century. Herder, who was influenced by Comte de Buffon's *Histoire naturelle* refused to separate the natural sciences from a history of man and raised similar doubts about what would become world history. He writes the following, pulling no punches in his criticism of the Eurocentrism of history based on absolute time (Iggers 1968: 35; Zammito 2009: 67):

"How foolish [it would be] for you to tarnish this ignorance and admiration, this imagination and reverence, this enthusiasm and child-sense with the *blackest devilry of your age*, with *fraud* and *stupidity, superstition* and *slavery*—to fabricate for yourself an army of *priest-devils* and *tyrant-ghosts* that exist only in your soul! A thousand times more foolish [still] for you magnanimously to bestow upon a child your *philosophical deism*, your *aesthetic virtue* and *honor*, your *universal love of all peoples* full of tolerant *subjugation, blood-sucking*, and *enlightenment* according to the high taste of your time!" (Herder 2004: 11).

Herder also has received renewed attention, possibly overcoming criticism for his emphasis on nation and race (as if nineteenth- and twentieth-century internationalism does not deploy racial hierarchies!), denial of objective criteria (Iggers 1968: 35), or "loose and hasty [thought]" (Collingwood 1994: 90).[3] Perhaps such dismissal of the nonmodern makes sense in an understanding of history that is filled with the superiority of the West, mechanistic desires, and notions of progress. Must we continue this masquerade?

For those of us who have studied the non-West through the poststructuralist and postcolonialist "turns," Herder's diatribe sounds familiar. Many of our historical subjects interrogated history as, to paraphrase Wiener (1950), traces (messages) of the past to reorganize (control) their societies. They tried to write their own histories within absolute time as a way to unify their territory around the idea of a nation and simultaneously to extract themselves from the locus of inferiority to the West. This very problem is an example of Althusser and Balibar's caution, the domestication of difference within a chronological structure that homogenizes. Many of Herder's ideas will sound familiar to those who have been seeking some common basis for understanding the diversity of the world by grounding human activity within people rather than abstract categories. People, language, and thought, he writes, are prior to philosophers and philosophy (Zammito, Menges, and Menze 2010: 673). One can see in this emphasis on activity prior to categories a connection to *historia magistra vitae*, where his history maintained a connection to human experience.[4] Herder's history still had remnants of communication in which it was related to the "life world" and the "reproduction of the social system" (Zammito, Menges, and Menze 2010: 673). From this prioritization of human thought and action and his connection of the science of man with that of nature, he recognized that peoples (races) have different characteristics and their development is conditioned by their biology—both body and environment.[5] We must ask how it is that two centuries later, Herder's invective still resonates. Progress?

My interest is not to resuscitate these men. Like my previous chapters, I use the methods of an historian to begin with a modest suggestion: rather simply, that we use dating systems of the unit or culture. On the surface, this operation honors the time system of the unit of analysis. It moves us toward an understanding of temporalities where times are both internal and possibly external to the activities of individuals, groups, communities, nations. But like my entrance into the digital humanities, it leads one toward first principles. The masquerade of what had been "common sense" is exposed to be cultural and ideological. This initial step opens up the possibility to accomplish Certeau's call to dehistoricize our objects of research. We see the selection that occurred, obscuring some of the "old," and the ignorance or dismissal of ideas from the "new" sciences. Increasingly, questions about the operations of diverse organisms, the centrality of information, the roles of observers, and the variability of pasts to understand outcomes appear in a very different light.

Historians have long endeavored to convey accurately pasts to current and future generations. This book shares this ideal but argues that it is key to avoid, not tacitly accept, the structures and limitations imposed by absolute time. History can be more than knowledge about past places; it can also be a tool for communication and understanding. I start by arguing for a shift from time to times. This shift sounds simple, but the plural is not additive; it questions the external and naturalized status of classical time. It can be the beginning of an inquiry into the very components of history—the duration, the unit of analysis, the role of the observer, and the multiple perspectives within data. No doubt there are other things we can do, but I hope to show that from this rather simple move, first principles come to light and help in the spring cleaning that Elias called for almost fifty years ago.

I end this chapter with a brief discussion of uncertainty.

INVERSION TO TIMES

A polite query to the title of this book has occasionally been, "So what is a history without time?" This conflation of time and chronology is the crux of the problem: chronology is but one form of time—in Certeau's words, an "alibi of time." Interestingly, a discipline that operates using time and prides itself on its ability to describe change has failed to keep abreast of changes to our understanding of time over the past century. Instead, absolute time has remained one of the most important and now an unconscious technology for communication in modern society; clock and chronological times have become so naturalized that often we don't realize how much it orients us to itself through synchronization and coordination rather than helping us understand organic processes. The proliferation of books on how modern society is accelerating and how to manage time (usually by becoming more efficient and thereby further burrowing oneself in mechanical time) are indications of the naturalization of chronological time.[6] Histories without chronology, then, are not without time or order; they are accounts of pasts that recognize the times that emerge through the activity of people. The shift from time to times is an inversion of an external time and internal times. I prefer this question: What is history using times?

It doesn't take much to show that time is multiple. Fraser (1987) discusses the times of physics,[7] biotemporality, nootemporality, and sociotemporality. Biotemporality brings in the various rhythms of organisms and societies; again, we are reminded of Wiener's emphasis on variety. Nootemporality is the human apprehension of time, the mental present. Fraser connects this to the *umwelt*, the physical and conceptual environment that makes up that mental present, and I would also include how people experience time.[8] The idea of the *umwelt* underscores the situatedness of objects, people, and understanding as well as the limitations and participation of the observer. Sociotemporality is the particular system people formulate to make sense of their world. This is where I would locate chronological time; it is but one way, albeit our naturalized way, to coordinate, organize, produce, and maintain values.

The inversion of time and times exposes the problem of linearity, of the replacement of one time with another. Instead, we need to untangle both so-called natural times and human apprehensions of time; heterogeneous times help us shift from time as a metric to times as a way of understanding the how and of manifold ways of behaving; it helps us recover human activity, relationality, and experience.

Internal Times

One rather simple adjustment is to record our writings about the past in the reckoning systems of the people or society we are describing. This is especially apparent for those working on non-Western or nonmodern societies, but more broadly it signals a conceptual shift from an understanding of pasts based on external, universalistic time to a time internal to some community or activity system. Certainly, using local dating systems might be disorienting; it makes it more difficult for us to emplot those societies within our understanding of cultures and communities across the globe. That is the point: they remain alter rather than other—that is, it is more difficult to locate them using the gesture of exclusion.[9] Peoples in the past and today often use multiple time systems simultaneously; scholars can too. Moreover, in today's digital environment, electronic aids (such as notes, mouse overs, and so on) are rather easy to incorporate. The point here is not to sow confusion or to claim something "new," but the disorientation suggests the extent to which the "simple" translation of dates into BC/AD[10] and the Gregorian calendar alters understanding and relations, fostering Whitehead's "fallacy of misplaced concreteness" (1925: 58). This disorientation inverts Foucault's "violence of time," where the expectation of translation and transmutation shifts to our, not their, responsibility.[11]

Historians have long struggled to study pasts without prejudging them, but that goal operates within a structure that already judges. Reflexivity has not sufficed. Historians do include some milieu in our work; we usually call it context. But what we call context emerged along with the birth of the past. It too is a part of the inversion that occurred to compensate for the schism that resulted when objects and happenings were filtered, abstracted, and transmuted through emplotment onto chronological time.[12] When pasts became prior and different, the extraction of objects and documents from the milieu that had given them meaning necessitates the application of context, the reinsertion of surroundings.[13]

By using the reckoning system of an activity that gives rise to happenings, documents, objects, and place, these become meaningful in the relations and connections of their specific site. This inverts emphasis to the activity, which might give rise to boundaries and meaning or the place and ideas of people. Time-reckoning systems often give us hints of the significant markers of that society—in Koselleck's words, a "space of experience." These systems in so-called backward places were often very sophisticated. For example, on Java, a five-day week and seven-day week operate simultaneously (Boellstorff 2007b: 238–41), and in 1900 Beirut, two systems for counting hours and several calendrical systems (Gregorian, Julian, Hijiri, and Ottoman) coexisted (Ogle 2015: 120–32). In short, these are systems (many societies had several) that help us understand the conceptual world of people, their understandings of previous happenings, and how they related to each other and to outsiders.

An implication for understanding this situatedness of pasts is evident in a story from Thomas Kuhn, recalling his effort to examine the connection of Aristotle with Galileo on mechanics. Kuhn (1977: xi–xii) reports that he was initially dumbfounded on how "simply wrong" Aristotle was on motion in comparison to his other observations, especially in biology and political behavior. Yet when he realized that Aristotle was concerned with qualities not states— that is, when he considered the conceptual understanding of Aristotle's epistemology, the "contemporary configuration on which it is dependent"—he understood not Aristotle's ignorance but a different way of appreciating pasts.

While my discussion of units thus far has generally followed history's use of nation or culture, those familiar with some form of complexity theory will see in this inversion the space for the emergence of groupings from simple agents and the interaction of these groupings into larger units and eventually to nation-states and beyond.[14] Lefebvre describes this hierarchical relational system: "The outcome is that the living body can and must consider itself as an interaction of organs situated inside it, where each organ has its own rhythm but is subject to a spatio-temporal whole. Furthermore, this human body is the site and place of interaction between the biological, the physiological (nature) and the social (often called cultural), where each of these levels, each of these dimensions, has its own specificity, therefore its space-time: its rhythm" (2004: 81). I will discuss units of analysis more below, but here it is important to point out that focusing on activity turns attention to the ways of behaving and interaction of agents and groupings.

Histories that use time-reckoning systems, that retain "a contemporary configuration on which it is dependent," are, interestingly, closer to pre-Newtonian chronologies (Jordheim, forthcoming) as well as to twentieth-century science, Einstein's *Eigenzeit*, and Fraser's and Bertalanffy's *umwelt*. They are not the same, but they share an important principle, that time is a "local, internal feature of the system of observation, dependent on observers and their measurements" (Adam 1990: 55–56). This use of an internal time shifts the way we understand pasts from a mechanical knowledge of how places became what they are to an understanding of human activity that gives rise to places. It is also a shift that inverts the standard temporal and spatial categories of modern history—the notion of duration and the units of analysis.

Duration

In the introduction to their edited book, Chris Lorenz and Berber Bevernage (2013) point to a seemingly contradictory feature of modern history. As time is unified, the writing of history depends on a fragmentation of that time. Past, present, and future is one way to break up time; periodization is a form of classing the past. These are examples of how Newtonian duration—between two moments—spatializes time. It goes further; the basic periodization—ancient, medieval, modern—also emerges with the Enlightenment. We are increasingly familiar with the performativity of such historical periodization, especially its Eurocentrism and Western frame (see, for example, Lorenz 2017; Nowotny 2016). This partitioning of time is another way that time structures and orients. Its systemic quality is backgrounded; it emphasizes the particular character of a place as it progresses, moving attention away from human activity (Lorenz 2017; Le Goff 2015). Bergson describes the way time obscures through the words that science uses: "time" and "motion," he argues, have eliminated duration and mobility ([1913] 2001: 120). I will discuss mobility in the next chapter. The distinction, for Bergson, between time and duration is between a quantitative (measurement) and qualitative (mental synthesis) understanding of human activity. The conflation of duration with classical time is a spatialization of time, the emplotment of successive moments (necessarily spatial), bounded by dates. This is the fragmentation of time and is most evident in the historical debates over the beginning and end date of a period.[15]

Bergsonian duration is a qualitative state in which past and present are not distinguished. He writes, "Pure duration might well be nothing but a succession of qualitative changes, which melt into and permeate one another, without precise outlines, without any tendency to externalize themselves in relation to one another, without any affiliation with number" (Bergson [1913] 2001: 104). White's account of the Troubles in his *Remembering Ahanagran* is an example of this pure duration. Using times as an integral element of the activity of people opens up the possibility of historicizing "our research in placing it back into a contemporary configuration on which it is dependent" (Certeau 2015: 9). Technology and quantitative measures are no longer the de facto metric. Instead, this notion of duration prioritizes activity.

Fernand Braudel (1980) and more recently Koselleck have tested the limits of Newtonian duration. Both suggest layered temporalities. In Braudel's case, it is the scales of geology and the environment of the earth, social scales, and individual scales; Koselleck divides these temporalities into transcendent structures (recurring biological cycles), repetitive structures (social forms), and singularities (event-like happenings; Koselleck 2018: 3–9; Olsen 2012: 226–31). I will discuss the potential and limitations of these layered temporalities in the next chapter. Here, I will focus on the difficulty of conceiving of history apart from the homogenizing structure of classical time. Braudel certainly recognized the difficulty of his proposal for history: "For the historian, accepting the *longue durée* entails a readiness to change his style, his attitudes, a whole reversal in his thinking, a whole new way of conceiving of social affairs" (1980: 33). Periodization (Newtonian duration) has remained dominant, and despite the respect of historians for his work and the frequent invocation of the *longue durée*, that "whole new way" remains on the horizon.[16] The uptake (or lack thereof) of this idea recalls Althusser and Balibar (1970); it shows the way that absolute time dominates and limits the historical imagination. This is evident in two recent or "new" (and important) periodizations—Big History and the Anthropocene—and two recent books that argue for a reevaluation of the boundaries of historical periods: Jacques Le Goff's tantalizingly titled *Must We Divide History into Periods?* (2015) and Jo Guldi and David Armitage's wonderfully provocative *The History Manifesto* (2014).

New periodization holds out a hope to alter how we understand pasts. Periodization, however, is a common way that chronological time has been "broken up" (Lorenz and Bevernage 2013). Each of the above ideas and scholars makes a proposal that is important to broadening the understanding and use of time in history, and each shows the powerful hold of chronological time. Big History alters our historical horizon by extending history backward to the Big Bang; it shows how minute human, let alone modern, history is. Classical time is still the basis, now extended backward.[17] The Anthropocene is a proposal to recognize a new geological period, and its potential is to reintegrate recent human activity with natural history, especially geologic changes (Zalasiewicz et al. 2011; Steffen et al. 2011; and Chakrabarty 2009).[18] The potential of the Anthropocene is to change the subject from human-centered to earth-centered history. One can imagine two times or histories, the earth's and humanity's, that are parallel, maybe even converging. Yet for many, the Anthropocene claims status by merging these two histories. As Chakrabarty notes in discussions of this era, especially in the social sciences and humanities, "world time" (what I call chronological time) prevails. He writes, "It is clear why it happens, for the science of Earth systems history has been made possible by the same technologies that have also produced, mapped, and measured the deleterious impact on the biosphere of the complex of species and life-forms represented by humans, their dependent or co-evolving living entities, and their technology" (2018: 25). This reminds me of Althusser and Balibar's criticism (1970).

The power of chronological time is also evident in efforts to revise history. Le Goff's essay follows more traditional historical methods, raising questions about the boundaries of periods. He has traces of sympathy for Bergson's duration when he argues that the medieval and early modern periods are filled with areas where there is an interpenetration of inherited and new forms and that the two periods should be merged. However, he is reluctant to relinquish the homogenizing order of absolute time (Le Goff 2015: 113–16); the chronological system remains, as does the gesture of exclusion, though the boundary between new and old shifts. Guldi and Armitage invoke Braudel's *longue durée* to point to new interpretive possibilities available in the digital technologies. In particular, they argue that data intensive tools can be used to process large databases that might excavate new patterns of past activity that have been obscured in traditional time units. An example (but not based on Big Data) of the potential of an extended time unit, what Braudel calls the social scale, is Marilyn Young's (2012) recent suggestion that twentieth-century US history is but one long war.[19] Each proposal is important in getting us to think about time beyond the chronological periods common to history, yet each shows the hold of the time of Newton and Hegel; the masquerade, the naturalization of time into a classified world system, remains powerful.

As Chakrabarty (2018) suggests, adjustments will be partial at best; it is important to move beyond classical physics toward a time as a part of life processes (this is the earth-centered approach proposed by Zalasiewicz et al. 2011). This shift from the physical to the biological is the potential of Anthropocene time, and it recalls Fraser's statement in the epigraph of the introduction: "[Time] has its origins in the life process" (1987: 4). Even though it has been difficult to escape these confines of absolute time, Whitehead suggests that it might not be as hard as we think—we already practice it:

> Every location involves an aspect of itself in every other location. Thus every spatiotemporal standpoint mirrors the world.
>
> If you try to imagine this doctrine in terms of our conventional views of space and time, which presuppose simple location, it is a great paradox. But if you think of it in terms of our naive experience, it is a mere transcript of the obvious facts. You are in a certain place perceiving things. Your perception takes place where you are, and is entirely dependent on how your body is functioning. But this functioning of the body in one place, exhibits for your cognisance an aspect of the distant environment, fading away into the general knowledge that there are things beyond (1925: 91–92).

Whitehead is describing the situatedness of our lives. We can also apply embeddedness to historical inquiry, but to do so, we need to unlearn (dehistoricize) our current structures. Historians can learn from work on cognition. For example, Connolly writes, "Human thinking in general involves complex culture/body/brain networks, and each level in this layered, tripartite assemblage is marked by specific capacities of speed, reception, and enactment"

(2002: 63). This approach is consistent with recent scholarship on cognition and learning. In psychology, Lev Vygotsky wrote about the "zone of proximal development" and proposed a "culturo-historical activity theory" (1978: 19–57, 84–91) as a conception of learning that is social; it considers the level of the learner, the social and cultural environment, and the particular conditions in which interaction occurs.[20] In the cognitive sciences, Edwin Hutchins (1995) has argued that cognition is "distributed"—that is, cognitive acts involve a distribution of signals from the brain, from the environment, from other people, and from mnemonics.[21] In anthropology, Dorothy Holland (1998) has proposed "figured worlds" as a way to think of the interaction between environment and individuals in cognitive processes. These and more show the complex relations in any single event, record, or observer: that reading, memory, orality, learning, and indeed, communication are conditioned by the social and physical environment and media as well as the mental state of individuals.

For a more prosaic (historical) example, we can turn to Carlo Levi's exile to southern Italy in 1935.[22] It is an account of exile of a doctor from Milan (Levi [1947] 2006) and his interaction with its rural inhabitants who had not yet been integrated into the time-order of modern society. We see that the past is not separate but repeats as a part of the present; what had happened is mean-ingful not because it is past but because it is a recurring part of life. One can read these encounters as modern sensibilities con-fronting people who will eventually "catch up." Yet as the story continues, it is unclear who is more advanced during 1930s Italy. The story becomes less about Levi than the community into which he was exiled.

In Levi and this community, we witness the conjunction of these different time scales (using Braudel's or Koselleck's layers, I see those of the earth and environment, social times, and various individual times); they conjoin in the moments of police action, immigration, and Levi's forced encounter with their daily life. The focus is on activity, relationships, and adjustments; perspective and expectations are highlighted. In the duration of the community, we see the specificity—the conditions, sensibilities, and limitations—of the lives of people prior to any determination of value. It gives us a sense of the different flows, the segmentation (not disconnection) of communities in fascist Italy, and a disconnect that is almost autonomy in a totalitarian system. In the places of conjunction, we see the repetitive dynamics of a people seeking to maintain equilibrium—the stability of the community. Change takes many forms beyond the forward motion of progress; change is evident in deviations from repetition. The layering of times in this passage helps us approach Braudel's proposal of a *longue durée*. This layering will be discussed in the following chapter.

Units of Analysis

The standard unit for segmenting pasts in classical time has been the nation-state. As I have shown in chapter 2, this form of historical understanding itself is historical, a rather recent way of ordering the globe. But just as a different notion of duration inverts our attention to activity, internal temporalities increase the possibility of units of analysis based on activity, not places. Jean Lave and Etienne Wenger have proposed "communities of practice," especially related to learning activities (1991: 98–100). Tim Ingold calls this the "taskscape," where action and interaction make up what he calls a "landscape" (1993: 163–64). In second-order cybernetics or complex systems, this is the self-organizing system or emergent form. In geography, this can be the notion of place, as opposed to a more abstract space. Each is rooted in some coalescence of activity of people rather than the geocultural units that make up the world. Many places might (and indeed do) interact to compose a nation-state, but they might also be autonomous from it, and they need not be a physical place (e.g., the virtual communities on the web). In history, a fine example is Paul Glennie and Nigel Thrift's (2009) focus on practices in their rich archival study *Shaping the Day*, an account of the reckoning of time in England and Wales between 1300 and 1800. They show how communities of practice, where people communicate information, share material and tools, and foster change or technological development are effective units for historical inquiry.[23] Repetition and positive (or negative) feedback can lead to growth (or decline), a new direction, or improvements in the practice. Glennie and Thrift identify such communities in the family (organizing family and household labor), market (determining the trading period in the market and setting curfew for tapsters and innkeepers in medieval Bristol), the city (opening the gate and scheduling meeting times), a particular knowledge (such as clock making), or an occupation (such as on a ship).

From this approach, Glennie and Thrift show how chronological accounts skew history toward the technological. They argue against E. P. Thompson's classic essay (1967) on industrial time and show that clock time as a means of regulating work was not new with industrialization but developed slowly over a long period from the fourteenth century. They also deemphasize the "genius" inventor and focus on the social processes by which ideas circulate as a key factor in invention and innovation. In their chapter on John Harrison, the winner of the Longitude Prize, Glennie and Thrift argue that he was less a "lone genius" than a person who combined several communities of practice: knowledge of general science and technology circulating in his region; a community circulating knowledge—manuscripts, texts, lectures—about clocks, craft, and theory of clock making; and connections to key figures (Glennie and Thrift 2009: chap. 10). This argument does not detract from the inventor, but it does caution us against fetishizing the new, "neophilia."[24] When we think of practice and use, we might instead see the ubiquity and importance of "old" technologies, despite the attention to the "new" (Edgerton 2007). Finally, Glennie and Thrift show the importance of considering earlier "medieval" society on its own terms, rather than as a lack (gesture of exclusion) of the modern. Even though these communities did not practice time as we do, they were often keenly concerned about time and timekeeping. To translate these out of history occults the ethical thinking that is so much a part of the human experience in favor of mechanical processes.

The simple adjustment to dates that use the time-reckoning system of record begins an inversion of our understanding of time and human activities. It brings out a lesson I learned from the digital humanities—to adapt Jerome McGann (2001), it exposes the imprecision in our thinking using chronological time.[25] From this recognition, history shifts from a knowledge of the past as a part of productive systems to an inquiry into human activity as a way to understand relations, processes, and experience. Paradoxically, this understanding of times as internal to activities strike me as closer to Ranke's *wie es eigentlich gewesen* (as it actually was).

APPROPRIATION: OBSERVERS, INFORMATION, AND STORIES

When invoking this phrase from Ranke, the neutral, perhaps even omniscient, position of the historian comes to mind. But this understanding of the situatedness of pasts moves us to another first principle; it makes the observer an integral, not external, part of any process—the source from which "facts" emerge as well as the scholar making sense of pasts. Objectivity cannot exist. Again, this is not new—Nietzsche's "On the Uses and Disadvantages of History for Life" (1983) comes to mind. This is an issue where history must decide if it is to work with contemporary understandings of time or remain in classical time.[26] The question of the observer was, of course, raised by Einstein—measurement and observation is relative to the observer. Most historians acknowledge the limitation of objectivity in private but are especially troubled when the methodologies that rely on it are called into question. Fears of subjectivity and relativism arise. But before knees jerk, a caution is in order: Bertalanffy, citing Einstein's special relativity, writes, "The absolutistic conception of earlier times and of classical physics is replaced by a scientific relativism" (1968: 227). Relativity is not countered by objectivity; it is the norm.

Special relativity is at odds with the monological framework and perspective of chronological history. It recognizes situatedness as well as heterogeneity. An approach that incorporates this variability is proposed by Certeau in the second volume of *The Mystic Fables*. He proposes appropriation as the central mechanism in an encounter between an inherited knowledge (tradition) and a present (2015: 98). Appropriation focuses on information—not facts—to discern how people used, interpreted, and understood things; it is an act of reading and interpretation. Heterogeneity is presumed; change (no matter how small or major) is built in. In every act of appropriation, there is a variation from what preceded. Appropriation recognizes sequence, but it is not necessarily linear. It is not characterized by replacement, from primitive to complex or old to new. Recursivity and feedback loops are just as possible as forward movement. If every reading is a question of how information is used, the question shifts toward how people build from, on, or against inherited forms of knowledge and practice. In appropriation, "history" takes on an additional significance beyond a description of how people acted. It is an actant itself; it is a part of the inherited forms of practice and understanding that filter how people receive information. We bring back historical understanding, not just of a past but also as a form of knowledge and understanding that is a part of the events of history.[27]

Appropriation coincides with recent studies on cognition that demonstrate how reading, memory, learning, and indeed, communication are conditioned by the social, cultural, historical, and physical environment, as well as the mental state of individuals. In my text, I call this situatedness. I have already mentioned Vygotsky's culturo-historical activity theory, Hutchins's distributed cognition, and Holland's figured worlds. In psychology, Maryanne Wolf describes recent research on reading that shows the importance of environment, preconceptions, and current thinking in how a text is read: "Reading is a neuronally and intellectually circuitous act, enriched as much by the unpredictable directions of a reader's inferences and thoughts, as by the direct message to the eye from the text" (2008: 16). If every reading—those of our historical figures as well as current historians—reuses the text, the application of facile anachronistic categories too must be interrogated as historical, not assumed. The past, tradition, habits, culture, and historical knowledge are all agents in the filtering and acquisition of information. In this sense, the past is not distant and different but a part of the present and changes depending on the understanding of the actors at that moment. History moves beyond a form of knowledge to also emphasize relations and communication.

Reading, situatedness, and distributed cognition all raise questions about the neutrality of the observer. This issue was evident in the discussions at the Macy Conferences even though it was rarely directly discussed.[28] The participants focused on human activity, especially interpretation, learning, perception, and semiotics. Some of the papers touched on perception, both psychological and physiological (through the frog's eyes), language and symbolism, humor, emotions, and communication patterns in humans and animals. In the end, the variation of such human activity was a big hurdle, and participants could not merge humans and machines into a new epistemology.

The observer reappears in cybernetics when von Foerster, a member of the conference, founded second-order cybernetics. In a later reminiscence, he describes this issue in a rather matter of fact but powerful phrase: "Anything said is said *by* an observer." He calls this Humberto Maturana's Theorem Number One and follows it with Heinz von Foerster's Corollary Number One: "Anything said is said *to* an observer" (von Foerster [1979] 2003: 283). In short, the observer is an actant, participant, and reporter. Here, I return to the significance of Fraser's nootemporality or Einstein's

Eigenzeit, the physical and conceptual environment that makes up that mental present, or proper time. The observer, the understanding during the moment of eruption, the language of bodies, the places of writing, and, of course, the moment of interaction all affect meaning. Bertalanffy, invoking the *umwelt*, writes, "It essentially amounts to the statement that, from the great cake of reality, every living organism cuts a slice, which it can perceive and to which it can react owing to its psycho-physical organization" (1968: 227).[29] The psycho-physical organization is the cultural-historical understanding, cognitive state, and material conditions of the perceiving person. It is, perhaps, reappearing. Recent musing about the direction of artificial intelligence sounds eerily similar to this gap that opened up in the latter part of the Macy Conferences. For example, Gary Marcus sees the AI strength in closed-end classification problems, but among its struggles are open-ended inference, commonsense reasoning, and a nonstable environment (2018).[30] In an appraisal of AI, the computer scientist Michael I. Jordan argued for the need of what he calls provenance—"Where did the data arise, what inferences were drawn from the data, and how relevant are those inferences to the present situation?" (2018).

In a sense, these questions are a part of the historian's toolkit, but they also push history beyond context to the situatedness of information. This mode of analysis not only builds from but also alters the role of the historian; in my mind, it makes that role more important. This situatedness also alters how we approach evidence. Documents and recorded happenings were and are not as fixed as we tend to think[31]; they are composed through their surroundings—they are situated. This recognizes a fundamental difference in understanding between recent and classical science—the impossibility of complete knowledge. For example, Bertalanffy writes, "All our knowledge, even if de-anthropomorphized (abstracted as 'fact' or data), only mirrors certain aspects of reality. . . . Any statement holds from a certain viewpoint only, has only relative validity, and must be supplemented by antithetic statements from opposite points of view" (1968: 248). The rise of digital media, especially through the rise of databases and the isolation of bits of information, is increasingly showing the need for this relationality of the document: "Every document, every moment in every document, conceals (or reveals) an indeterminate set of interfaces that open into alternate spaces and temporal relations" (McGann 2001: 181). Interpretation and variation of understanding of events is the norm; whether events happened or not is not questioned.

I would argue that events gain stability when the document is recognized as a part of a network of appropriation. Sources, or "facts," are no longer objects that exist, isolated from the milieu of their becoming. Historical arguments become less about which fact is correct and should be emphasized or ignored and more about what the relationships and meanings are that emerge in the use of information. This is relevant for historical objects and events as well as for the historian. People then used information embedded in documents in their interpretations, decisions, and actions. Historians do the same. This is where Certeau's argument that texts and documents constitute a theater is especially relevant. When documents are considered as a theater or nodes of activity, they occur among different actors with varying inscriptions and differing forms. We have heard this before—for example, from Bakhtin; it bears repeating, not forgetting or exorcising through claims to disciplinary purity. This variability of interpretations of the same event was brilliantly depicted in Akira Kurosawa's well-known movie *Rashomon* (1950). He shows how individuals appropriate what they see, and this differs depending on the past and experience of each person. We open the possibility of extending history beyond what is, to how people communicate and ways of behaving.

Appropriation also facilitates the opening up of the past, closed off by focus on the document, to include traces of relations, ideas, and sensibilities of various peoples. Here historians need to ask whether disregarding pasts that don't have evidence based on documents and "simple location" has turned attention away from experience and relations and consequently restricts history's significance, even more in a more interactive, electronically interconnected world. For example, the life-history approach in archaeology is an example of how fixed or "dead" artifacts change through appropriation. Cornelius Holtorf (1996) has shown how peoples at different times make sense of megaliths. These monuments are not static (people destroy, move, repurpose, historicize, and display them), and their meanings often shift depending on the community at a particular time. In this case, appropriation uses the time system of the unit—that is, the contemporary society—rather than some external temporality. Unlike the case of *Rashomon*, where there are multiple interpretations of a singular event, heterogeneity is in the variation of meanings (or forgettings) that are attributed to this site as a part (perhaps but not necessarily a past) of the present.

Stories, we should remember, were expunged from the archive as history and literature were defined, and historians have since worked to recover bits and pieces. In his famous essay "The Storyteller," Benjamin laments a result of this shift, the decline of storytelling: "It is as if something that seemed inalienable to us, the securest among our possessions, were taken from us: the ability to exchange experiences" (1968a: 83). There have been periodic attempts to reintegrate the everyday into history; two notable efforts are the AHA presidential addresses of Carl Becker (1932) and William Cronon (2013). Much of Certeau's *The Mystic Fable* engages with evidence that has been relegated to the margins or beyond of history—storytelling, oral transmissions, visuality, the body, and the senses. Each is an important mode of communication that leaves traces for thinking about relations, transmission, interaction, and transmutation among people. The purpose of the story, Benjamin writes, "is not concerned with an accurate concatenation of definite events, but with the way these are embedded in the great inscrutable course of the world" (1968a: 96).

For my purpose, attention to storytelling goes beyond gripping accounts of past events and people. Stories are also a way to bring together varying accounts and perspectives. David Herman points out how storytelling, particularly through embedded narratives, involves several voices and perspectives that encourage sense-making. It "affords structure for human understanding—more specifically, for the distribution of mind across time frames, spatial locales, and contexts of social interaction" (2013: 271). Harold Innis reminds us of the connection of the book and the essay to classical time: "The use of a medium of communication over a long period will to some extent determine the character of knowledge to be communicated" (1951: 34). In other words, perhaps the long-form print narrative has locked history into a classical time that abstracts our accounts of people beyond recognizable experience.

Print media are certainly not dead; they have certain affordances. Now we have tools to also "write" history differently, and this can impact how we understand pasts and history. This potential was suggested by Fasolt, who differentiates the thinking of Bartolus of Sassoferrato from modern history. The modern is categorical and singular while "for Bartolus it was but the general form of distinctions dividing the commonwealth into a manifold of subordinated spheres of thought and action . . . all of them were held together by a fine-grained structure of differentiation and relation" (2004: 203). This recalls Lefebvre's *Rhythmanalysis* (2004). The affordances of new media for writing what Bakhtin might call a dialogic history can help us think and write history using multiple, not just one, distinction(s).

The graphic novel, for example, offers the simultaneity of different perspectives—narrative and experiential—that complement and challenge historical forms like chronology, causality, and linearity.[32] Individual cells of the comic often contain multiple perspectives and motion; multiple voices that visualize experience, verbal and embodied; pages that depict multiple and layered temporalities; and varied pacing.[33] For history, they also offer the possibility of combining "major events" with the activity of people operating among those events, and Hillary Chute argues that comics are a growing and well-suited genre for the documentary of trauma (2016: 14). Chute turns to remarkably powerful works like Art Spiegelman's *Maus*, Keiji Nakazawa's oeuvre on the Hiroshima atomic bombing, and the reporting of Joe Sacco in his *Palestine*. Mizuki Shigeru's four-volume *History of Showa* is both history and autobiography; it offers a "normal" history of Japan from 1926 to 1989 and his life experience as a youth in the 1930s, a foot soldier in Papua-New Guinea, an overworked laborer during the postwar period, and finally a celebrated author. The "facts" of Japanese history look different when situated within these experiences than in the standard histories; the story questions imperialism, violence of officers toward soldiers, and the anomie of the postwar years (reminiscent of Robert Musil's *The Man without Qualities*).

Divisions between the historical and fiction are blurred. Spiegelman challenged the categorization of *Maus* as fiction; he raises the possibility that something is "historically true in essence, but not strictly factual" (Toni Morrison, quoted in H. White 2014: 22). The historian William Steele, who possesses an encyclopedic understanding of popular material in nineteenth-century Japan, wrote an account of Goemon during the events of the Meiji *ishin*. Goemon did not exist, but his activity is based on an extensive reading of the broadsheets circulating at the time. Is this fiction? Nakazawa's manga on Hiroshima and the atomic bomb, Spiegelman's *Maus*, the reporting of Joe Sacco, and other media broaden pasts that fill our understanding of our present. These raise questions about the historical.

Stories are a way to confront history, to reengage parts of experience that have been marginalized. Benjamin writes, "The wisest thing—so the fairy tale taught mankind in olden times, and teaches children to this day—is to meet the forces of the mythical world with cunning and with high spirits. . . . The liberating magic which the fairy tale has at its disposal does not bring nature into play in a mythical way, but points to its complicity with liberated man" (1968a: 102). The mythical world that stories confront can be history as myth. I read the complicity of nature and the liberated man as a disavowal of the various dichotomies that constitute modern society. I return to the mechanical or quantitative bias of absolute time and the need for biological times. Nature is not separate (so that it can be exploited or used to disparage as primitive) from humans. When the boundary between past and present becomes blurred, the various specters and ghosts of the past (those entombed) can raise questions about the binaries—past/present, tradition/modern, old/new—on which the modern depends. For Benjamin, stories operate apart from the gesture of exclusion.

This is an opportunity for history to add to its conceptual and practical tool kit. We must recognize that history (the discipline) is declining in attention while history (in a broad sense) is very popular in print and electronic media (de Groot 2009). I am not arguing for the popularization or massification of the historical profession—uses of the past, though, are moving to areas beyond the traditional historian's reach. My point is that we must be aware of the confines of the Enlightenment system. For example, recent work in storytelling involves questioning both the linearity of communication from oral to written and opening the past to questions of human experience that had been denigrated. I have already discussed the latter, but the work of folklore specialist John Miles Foley (2012) suggests that we should also look for isomorphisms that have been distanced by chronology. He argues that recent digital media bear many similarities to oral traditions, especially in their topological natures.[34] This work suggests that over a long term of different modes of communication—oral, textual, and digital—narrative print text might be the outlier.

UNCERTAINTY?[35]

From a perspective of orthodox history, my call for a methodology rooted in a recognition of heterogeneity seemingly weakens certitude in historical interpretation and writing. Heterogeneous times, the relationality of interaction, the malleability of texts, the position of the observer in the activity, and the variability of reading make causal and facile conclusions more difficult. Moreover a similar interaction at a different place and time can lead to different outcomes. But we know, don't we, that history is reductive, always partial, and place does matter? Yet we adhere to our myths; and if the Anthropocene is dated from the steam engine, then these myths must be seen as an ideological foundation of the technocratic society in which we exist. I agree with Chakrabarty that the time of world history must change to tackle the problems of the climate change.

This approach, a history without chronology, does not bring greater uncertainty. I readily admit that I join Fraser (1987) in his caution about the time-compact order in the epigraph to the interlude. On the one hand, uncertainty already abounds in our current system, but it has been differentially placed in an ideology of order while blaming others for problems. But this displacement, as Harootunian suggests in the epigraph, has failed. It is time to recognize this heterogeneity that the gesture of exclusion has occulted. In one of his characteristically succinct yet playful essays, Heinz von Foerster writes, "I have no doubts that you share with me the conviction that the central problems of today are societal. On the other hand, the gigantic problem-solving conceptual apparatus that evolved in our Western culture is counter productive not only for solving but essentially for perceiving social problems." Historians and humanists can remain smug and read von Foerster's observation as a recognition of the limitation of science. It is, but it is more; von Foerster continues that the root cause for these "cognitive blind spots" are causation, deduction, and objectivity

(1979: 283–84). These are keywords of modern historical inquiry, of historical thinking, of our modern world. We circle back to the hidden base in chronological time that facilitated causation and objectivity as fundamental components, now root causes. These blind spots are (and continue to be) a source of our failure to encompass what we think we understand. This has been true throughout the twentieth century (rebellion and revolution were a part of the colonial edifice) and is perhaps even more pressing today as technologies for communication and for killing are reaching more and more people and the earth is changing faster than our institutions and policies. The others (even more, those who act against the conceptual confines) are the numerous specters that haunt our current understanding, and they seem to increase along with the inability of current categories to make sense of (and contain) the diversity of our world.

In Certeau's complex and remarkable study of mystics, he asks, "Out of their strangeness . . . can something be born?" (2015: 4). For Certeau, "mystics" is a stigmatized category, like inner city, immigrant, and those "behind." He recognizes the temporal distance, yet sees a similarity, which makes sense if we accept Simmel's separation of technological change and sociocultural stability (quoted in chapter 1). Without chronological time to measure old and new, we might learn from distant pasts as well as recent science. Serres argues for the similarity of Lucretius's writings on the motion of atoms and that of Jean Perrin (and by extension—quantum theory; Serres with Latour 1995: 48–52). More recently, Siegfried Zielinski (2006) turns to "deep time" to look for the new in the old. Both de Cusa and Bertalanffy were writing when the prevailing knowledge system, the church and classical science, lost their power for explanation and understanding. Both sought to formulate something else rather than to reiterate some comfortable mode of knowing. It seems that we too are in a moment when the existing system, absolute time, is decreasingly able to contain the world it claims to order. This is related to our current concern of time—presentism, fatal confusions, things out of sync, and questions about digital media. Strangeness is no longer the other; it seems to be in ourselves. What might be born is greater emphasis on qualities and relations; these are not far from Certeau's statement that "*mystics* does not have its own content: it is an exercise of *the other* in relation to a given *site*; it is characterized by a set of specific 'operations' in a field that is not its own" (2015: 22). Heterogeneity makes more possible inquiries that ask, following von Foerster, "What are the properties of an observer?"

To consider this question, historians already use perhaps the most important tool for addressing these issues—reading. Historical thinking requires skill in finding, filtering, interpreting, and encapsulating data and narratives. These skills are more important than ever in our digital age. But I am arguing for less a reading to absorb and know than one to also appropriate, communicate, and understand. It is a form of reading that inverts practices from knowing structures within which people and objects existed to understanding the ways people make sense of and engage with their surroundings. This practice is a form of reading that seeks a "way of doing" that constitutes the text and helps us understand ways of behaving.[36] Reading needs to be attuned less to the emplotment of data onto a grid of time and space and more to a recognition of the heterogeneous views of an object or event. In *Practices of Everyday Life*, Certeau emphasizes the variability of reading not just as information transmission but also as a way for readers to visit some other place. He writes, "The reader produces gardens that miniaturize and collate a world . . . but he, too, is 'possessed' by his own fooling and jesting that introduces plurality and difference into the written system of a society and a text" (1984: 173). If every reading—those of our historical figures as well as current historians—reuses the text, the application of facile anachronistic categories must be interrogated as historical, not assumed. Von Foerster's compact distinction—"It is how you say it," not "Say how it is"—is particularly apt (2014: 129). History can again be a form of understanding and communication as well as bodies of knowledge. It is by incorporating these varying views and perspectives that I believe we have a better understanding of pasts.

Finally, up to this point, my discussion on heterogeneity has only hinted at how these multiple units relate (or don't). It does, though, destabilize change as a linear description of becoming. Bergson writes, "The point is that usually we look at change but we do not see it. We speak of change, but we do not think about it. We say that change exists, that everything changes, that change is the very law of things: yes, we say it and we repeat it; but those are only words, and we reason and philosophise as though change did not exist. In order to think change and see it, there is a whole veil of prejudices to brush aside" (2002: 248–49). Again, we encounter the language of hiding—masquerade, veil, occult, and so on. This discussion on heterogeneity is important in itself, but it is necessary for my next chapter, to think anew about change. Serres writes, "The work of transformation is that of the multiple" (1995: 101).

CHAPTER FOUR

CHANGE AND HISTORY

At the heart of the Industrial Revolution of the eighteenth century there was an almost miraculous improvement in the tools of production, which was accompanied by a catastrophic dislocation of the lives of the common people.

—Karl Polanyi ([1944] 1957: 33)

If you imagine a change as being really composed of states, you at once cause insoluble metaphysical problems to arise. They deal only with appearances. You have closed your eyes to true reality.

—Henri Bergson (2002: 259)

In order to be able to accept change, time has to be created. In order to be able to accept changes with time, it could be continued, the categories of time have to be changed repeatedly.

—Helga Nowotny (2016: 50–51)

Perhaps the most unsettling question that a decentering of chronology and a framework that emphasizes heterogeneity raises is the ability of history, in contrast to claims, to discuss change. The modern discipline of history sees itself as study of change (Rüsen

1995: 120). Yet I am more and more convinced, after writing two books that sought (unsuccessfully) to move beyond a teleological history, that I also have been confined to the mythical structure. I discussed, through a lens that challenged some common understandings, how things came to be, not how change happens. History's concept of change is to describe (or critique) how units—nations, societies, and communities—became what we know them to be. Within a homogeneous time, we begin history from the end (usually the present) and move backward to some origin to discuss the unfolding toward that endpoint. The epigraph from Polanyi exhibits this pattern; the critique is important but reinforces the linear structure. I too complied.

I now believe that history is a field of knowledge that maintains states and conditions through a language of movement. In history, change is an external measure that too often, in Bergson's words in the epigraph, "deal[s] only with appearances."[1] The dislocations described by Polanyi, resulting from technological improvement, continue. This recalls Manuel's description (in an epigraph of chapter 2) of Newton's effort to write history—"quantities of geographical space in temporal sequence"—and Toews's observation that Hegelian rationality is a world of forms that do not reach the level that "make the shaping activity possible in the first place" (2004: 5). I read the "metaphysical problems" that Bergson refers to as states.[2] These states are "appearances," extracted from flows, that facilitate quantitative measure across dates (Adam 1990: 51). Historians call this "change over time."

The limitation of the concept of change in history is evident in a recent forum of the *American Historical Review* on "Explaining Historical Change" (Akyeampong et al. 2015). The panel was composed of important historians in their respective fields. The discussion traversed a rather sophisticated terrain, including hermeneutics and the impossibility of describing a "reality." Yet the whole seemed to return to the common denominator; the panel concluded with a reiteration of history as continuity and discontinuity; classical time remained the norm. It returned to the standards, goals, and metrics of existing units—the nation-state, eras, institutions, and identity—but with a critical edge. Within this system, change "occurs," and we feel more knowledgeable simply because the date is more recent—it is "new." This is the gesture of exclusion at work; an improved technology is applied (often reinforcing an existing practice), or simply the more recent is juxtaposed to something existing (now categorized as past).

In the previous chapter, I introduced Bergson's identification of *time* and *motion* as two words science uses as a "veil" and discussed how the notion of duration can be a way to conceive of time through human sensibility rather than mechanical processes. Here, I take up the second of his veils, the difference between motion and mobility. When I first became interested in temporality, I taught seminars on time and space. Among the readings, David Harvey (1996: 261) describes "permanence" as space carved from the flow of processes. History gives credence to the idea of the nation-state as a "permanence," as if it has always existed. Then motion and circulation are the principal ways to discuss movement—development and progress—within and among this permanence. It is important to point out that the purpose of this spatialization is certainty, organization, and control—in short, stability. I have been calling this spatialized time. The veil, the elevation of time and motion over duration and mobility, is to operate within these permanences as if they are external to rather than created from human activity. My switch from temporalities to times is my way of centering time as an internal part of activity.

Like duration, mobility provides a conceptual path to invert motion from movement between abstract externalities to activity that makes up units. Various forms of activity—extension, contraction, interaction, passing, recurrence, redundancy, and so on—are elements of the flow of processes. By focusing on such activity, the ordering systems become one, not the only, possibility. More important, the potential for conceiving of change moves more toward the qualitative conditions—the activity that comprises the unit—rather than the quantitative measurement of states.

From the mid-1990s, mobility—the "mobility turn" or "new mobilities paradigm"—has become a popular new subject or approach (Cresswell 2006: ix). It emerged more in anthropology and sociology; history has been slower to embrace it. Perhaps one reason that history has not as readily embraced mobility is because of its role in maintaining spatialized time through its focus on time and motion. Bruce Clarke's concise description of the difference between classical science and second-order cybernetics contrasts this difficulty; "one discovers that whereas circularity is death (by infinite regress) to *structures*, it is life (by autonomous self-regulation) to *systems*" (2009: 36). Movement is central to both, but descriptions within classical time presume forward movement that is juxtaposed to fixed forms, repetitive action, and dead "facts" that are contained by or move between forms. On the other hand, the mobility of organisms includes variability, process, and relations that are necessary for their existence. Recurrence is a basic activity of organisms from which interaction, growth, transformation, homeostasis, or decay occurs.

Tim Ingold aptly shows this difference through his description of how people operate rather than how they function within modern structures. He compares wayfaring and transport; the wayfarer moves along, taking in the surroundings, and inhabits that which he traverses. This is juxtaposed to the traveler, who moves across from point to point.[3] Ingold applies this formulation to narrative, and I would extend it to the historical discipline: "This fragmentation . . . has taken place in the related fields of *travel*, where wayfaring is replaced by destination-oriented transport, *mapping*, where the drawn sketch is replaced by the route-plan, and *textuality*, where storytelling is replaced by the pre-composed plot. It has also transformed our understanding of *place*: once a knot tied from multiple and interlaced strands of movement and growth, it now figures as a node in a static network of connectors"

(2007: 75). Wayfaring becomes a metaphor for recentering our understanding around human activity rather than in the categories that speak for and encompass them. It focuses on process, the recursivity where pasts are as much of the present as they are of the future. It makes possible lateral thinking—the transposition of ideas and tools from one place to another as processes of living rather than as prescriptions for the not-yet (the behind) to become like us. Place, then, is a part of the process rather than something preexisting. As in my discussion of duration, mobility enables us to envision the situatedness of the units and the encounter. Change is less the becoming of what we know than, first, the ways organisms, people, and environments operate, adapt, and use their specific conditions and, second, how these activities lead to larger and larger structures as well as interaction of larger units.

I ended the previous chapter with Bergson's questioning of our ability to see change. Bergson, in the epigraph, asserts that we have closed our eyes to true reality. We don't have to go as far as Bergson, and one must be suspicious whenever encountering the "really" or "truly" real. But this statement coincides with my account that history, when established (in the nineteenth century), was itself a "virtual reality," especially in comparison to what previously existed. It also aligns with Simmel's separation of material progress from sociocultural life and with increasing scholarship pointing toward a desynchronization (as if they ever were synchronized). The reality that we see has been refracted through a lens that abstracts and classes; that lens emphasizes the quantifiable, mechanical, and technological, and it simultaneously deemphasizes human sensibility.

Nowotny suggests a corrective: "Change, or a more fashionable word, transformation, is the normal state of natural and human affairs, exacerbated by the increasingly intricate interaction between humans and their environment" (2016: 38). This rather simple, but powerful, statement inverts—maybe even upends—our current thinking based on classical time; change is decoupled from chronological time. Instead, activity is the normative condition of organisms—nature, human, and social—which are constantly transforming and intricately interacting. Again, I recall Certeau's inversion to historicize our research and dehistoricize our objects of study. Change (as activity) is a constant; whether it is significant requires values, evaluation, and metrics. Perspective, environment, and goals are integral factors. To understand change apart from chronology, we might start from the complex interaction of humans with each other and with their environment.

Before discussing the ways that times can be used to understand such interactions, I will first return to entropy and biology. I mentioned these in chapter 1, but here I will emphasize how these times help us approach Nowotny's argument in the epigraph that "categories of time have to be changed repeatedly." If we do so, we broaden what might be historical: the past is not necessarily a dead past, people's sensibilities are important, transformation is local and situated, perspectives vary, ideas are constitutive of societies, and multiple times coexist.

TWENTIETH-CENTURY TIMES[4]

Entropy

Most social scientists and humanists who work on time see the clock as the metaphor for the modern world, and I too have generally followed this tendency. Yet Prigogine and Stengers (1984) distinguish Newtonian science—the clock—from the industrial age that was based on the burning of energy. This difference indicates that thermodynamics, especially the second law, has not been a significant component of the understanding nor of a critique of modern time.[5] Again, we are confronted by the mythical basis of our chronological system—it is true because we accept it, not because of a scientific basis. My use of entropy is to raise the need for a more complex understanding of times that become apparent when we recognize these laws.[6]

Interestingly, entropy, the idea that things move toward disorder, bears similarity to premodern forms of thinking where gods (or God) created the perfect world and human activity (history) by definition has been a devolution from that world. I do not mention this because I seek to return to some idealized past. Instead, we need to recognize that this earlier view, when placed alongside a more recent (late nineteenth century!) scientific understanding of energy, is not an outmoded notion—a dead past from which we have progressed. Instead, it points to the reductive or narrow range of analysis of mechanical processes based on Newtonian time that has ignored or obscured outcomes that are a constituent part of the very same process. The obscured or ignored outcomes become separate issues or lamentable problems, are categorized as waste, have unintended consequences, or are blamed as the fault of others. Linear time facilitates this occlusion through its focus on the new technological "innovation" and production—measurables.

Perhaps the most important aspect of entropy for social processes is that it forces us to recognize multiple outcomes from a single process. Jeremy Rifkin and Ted Howard write, "Many people think that pollution is a by-product of production. In fact, pollution is the sum total of all available energy in the world that has been transformed into unavailable energy. Waste, then, is dissipated energy" (quoted in Adam 1990: 62). All aspects of the process are important, and Adam writes that what had been waste becomes "a source of order and creativity" (1990: 64). When we open our fields to include all, not just desired, output, we see a much more complex relationship that might involve different time scales and times. There are many examples: we can turn to the burning of fossil fuels for energy and transportation, the generation of waste, the rise of pollution, and the changing geoclimatic system (Zalasiewicz et al. 2011; Gabrys 2011). Colonialism was a constituent, interactive part of modernity, not its effect (Harootunian 2007); and the global corporate traveler relies on a series of on-demand and low-wage workers (Sharma 2014). In these examples, what we have too often ignored, written off as externalities, or pitied and suggested aid for, are integral parts of the process. Entropy helps lift the veil. This connects to the epigraph from Polanyi and the statement from Simmel in that we must at minimum be specific on our subjects, and more important, recognize divergent outcomes, rates, and decay. Peter Wagner's recent effort to reconceive of progress similarly separates epistemic-economic progress from sociopolitical control (2016).

This incorporation of entropy upsets the very foundation of historical understanding. Newtonian mechanics and Hegelian development are inverted. We can no longer begin from a structure that celebrates the move from some originary, natural state toward civilization and order. The question is how long can we continue this myth; Sir Arthur Eddington warns, "If your theory is found to be against the second law of thermodynamics . . . there is nothing for it but to collapse in deepest humiliation" (quoted in Georgescu-Roegen 1986: 14). When applied to biological and social systems, from cells to large social systems, an exchange of energy is basic. The organism is never at rest (stasis), and instead, without active maintenance, it is degrading. Repetition and feedback loops (positive or negative) are central temporalities of the process, not some prior condition. Maintenance is necessary to keep a steady state, and in maintenance, change also occurs. In short, when we include thermodynamics, change becomes multilinear and complex; it is degradation, trade off, loss (high entropy), emergence, coevolution, and improvement. This helps us move toward an understanding of the epigraph from Bergson that change according to chronological time is that of appearances and that a system that recognizes the dynamics of organisms moves us closer to "true reality."

Circular Causality

If someone today were to propose the use of an abstract metric for mechanical motion to understand life processes, he would, at best, have a difficult time convincing us of its suitability; mechanical motion and life processes are "completely different" realms (Vester 1979: 53). Yet the conflation of life processes into mechanical motion is the legacy of classical science, which leads us to think of causality as linear and circularity as repetitive, a condition of stasis. This encounter between physical time and biological processes returns us to General System Theory (GST) and the Macy Conferences on cybernetics.[7] Both, from different sciences, turned to organic forms to formulate a richer and more complex conceptual system to study and understand physical, social, and life processes.[8] Just as the presence of entropy brings out the multiple outputs of a process and inverts directionality, the turn to biological systems inverts the basis of understanding of mobility and stability and presumes multidirectional and multitemporal movements.

In contrast to Newtonian motion, the basic unit of biological and social systems or the agent (the cell, the individual, the community, or the nation-state) is not at rest but is dynamic. Activity—repetition, dissipation, decay, recursion, feedback, and interaction—is constant. Purpose (what was often called teleology at the Macy Conference) varies, but importantly, it is local; it exists in the activity of the unit rather than as some conceptual ideal in the future. Finally, what we have understood as universal laws or "nature" (and which I have pointed out are historical forms— chronological time and history) are described here as secondary regulations. What we might call stability—homeostasis—is frequently the purpose rather than a negative of progress.[9]

While homeostasis suggests an equilibrium, it doesn't mean static or unchanging. This is where Koselleck's concept of layered times (discussed in chapter 3) is important; the second layer, the structure of repetition (social form), is a temporality within which the first layer, singularities (event-like happenings) emerge. Maintenance, decay, or something "new" emerges from repetition. For example, in his *Evolutionary History*, Edmund Russell describes how evolution happens through repetitive activity: "Evolution is ordinary, not exceptional. It happens all around (and inside) every one of us—you, me, and the dog next door—every day. We rarely notice it, but it shapes our lives continually" (2011: 5). This understanding returns to Darwin rather than Spencer's adaptation of evolution as human progress. This process is the regular cycles of organisms including reproduction—each organism has its own time, multiple organisms of different time scales coexist and interact, and coevolution happens at differential and barely perceptible rates. Russell's use of the word *continually* is an example of what I have called circular causality. This is where we move change beyond Newtonian states. Bertalanffy points to a key difference: mechanical processes are oriented toward "certain products or performances"; in contrast, "the order of process in living systems is such as to maintain the system itself" (1968: 78).[10] This is the difference raised by Vester. In human life, adaptation is a part of the process of living. Change is coevolutionary—the adaptation of one thing in reaction to another (say, an external stimulus) leads to the mutual adaptation of each; humans have fostered the changes of other organisms, which in turn continue to shape human history.[11]

The attentive reader will note the similarity to Gurevich in chapter 2, where he describes stability as a result of repetition: "The past, as it were, returns continuously, and this lends solidity, gravity, a non-transient character to the present" (1985: 143). My point is to emphasize the centrality of the process and activity that is involved rather than to emplot such behavior as some form of lessness, of incompleteness, or of ignorance. Change is constant; occurs at different, often very slow rates; is multiple; and is not limited to developmental or forward motion. Change can be degeneration, disorder, decay, or death. These are outcomes of entropy—gradual decay without input. Imagine the changes that would be necessary to maintain the global average temperature at what it is right now (which will be higher by the time you read this). Redundancy gives rise to patterns and commonalities (space), but encounters with different forms and changing environments generate feedback loops and lead to adjustment, adaptation, and learning (history). These processes require the exchange of information. Cybernetics (Shannon and Weaver 1949) also extended this notion of entropy to information theory.

This process elevates the significance beyond a description of some past. History, or historical understanding, plays several roles that go beyond description. People incorporate ideas and understand situations based on their conceptual systems (as well as the environment at that moment). Recorded happenings serve as information that systems, institutions, and individuals might filter into data or "facts." Historical knowledge, the learned understanding of the community, also filters information in the act of learning, interpreting, and decision-making, and the historian writes history based on the community as well as outside (including abstract) ideas and influence. That history then provides another filtering mechanism for recorded happenings. Repeat. History acts on past observers/actors/subjects as well as on our present.

This process is well beyond linear systems. The emphasis is on the various connections and relations that are parts of a process; Dupuy explains circular causality: "In a 'system' (that is to say, an organism), the laws of physics allow the individual elements a number of degrees of freedom. This indeterminacy at the lower level ends up being reduced by the constraints imposed upon it by the integrated activity of the whole—constraints that themselves result from the composition of elementary activities. The whole and its elements therefore mutually determine each other. It is this codetermination that accounts for the complexity of living beings" (2000: 136). This notion of circular causality contrasts with the repetition and cyclical forms of classical science. It does not eliminate change; instead, it helps emphasize the parameters, activity, interactions, and emergences of a system.

Dupuy's description points to what we today tend to know as a complex system. The basic units are heterogeneous and unique; a variety of actions are possible from their interaction. Mobility is constant; repetition, dissipation, reproduction, feedback loops, and interaction are central. Networks and assemblages are metaphors that have become common ways to think of nonlinear relations. Learning or adaptation is a central part of the interaction. The inversion is evident through von Foerster's distinction of change as trivial and nontrivial (see especially von Foerster 2014: 15–23). The former is linear cause and effect; the latter is multilinear and complex. In the latter, after each interaction, the qualitative state of actor and actant changes and the operation of the system changes. Nontrivial change helps us discern the problem of states and appearances in Newtonian mechanics. The various actors and actants shift and adjust; the next operation is different. This process is affected by and affects its environment. Each agent, its embodied condition, and each interaction is situated within a unique setting. This helps us get to the qualitative processes of human activity.

The variability of these interactions inverts our current system that marks and emplots variation onto an ideal or universalized geometric grid. Nowotny writes, "What makes complex systems complex are their multiple feedback loops and indirect cause-effect relations, which play out at different timescales and speed" (2016: 129). From this interaction of agents, new forms emerge. Emergence is not additive but a result of a combination that leads to something different, beyond the qualities of individual agents. These systems can be self-organizing—for example, urban systems or schools of fish—or they can be hierarchical, such as families and nations. Maintenance of the system through repetitive action is as important as "new" actions.[12] Emergence can be a recurrent process, or it can be an adaptation (evolution). Indeed, change might come from repetition itself or the failure of repetition rather than from some innovation that claims the new.

TURBULENT, CRUMPLED, TATTERED TIMES

So we understand that time is multiple and that we should focus on activity (duration to reconceive of time and mobility to reconceive of motion), incorporate entropy, and adjust to circular causality. What does it mean now to think historically? In a sense, this clarifies Benjamin's statement that objectivistic history is "the strongest narcotic of the century" (1999: 463). Simple location, linear causality, and a reduced archive produce and maintain a false certainty.

I hope it is clear that we need to recognize that classical time—unless we choose to follow a mythic notion—is one (albeit major) time of many that operate in our world. It is not easy to relinquish its centrality because our world, our conceptual systems, and our daily lives are organized around it, but the claimed certainty of linear history has produced an uncertain world. Again, this is not new. The more I have worked on this short book, the more I feel as if I am writing about a history of what has been forgotten in our craft of history, an amnesia that accompanies or is shrouded by Benjamin's narcotic. The power of this narcotic is borne out by the criticisms that existed as far back as the Enlightenment. Herder writes sarcastically, "Would that everything went in a nice *straight line*, with every *subsequent human being* and every *subsequent generation* being *perfected* according to *his* ideal in a *beautiful progression* for which he alone was able to provide the *highest exponent* of virtue and happiness!" (2004: 70–71). Thomas Carlyle complained in 1830 as chronological history was becoming popular, "Things done were not a series, but a group" (2002: 7). One can think of Braudel's *longue durée*, Foucault's archaeology, and more recently Harry Harootunian has shown how Marx's multiple and layered temporality was reduced into a linear Marxism. We end up with comments like Benjamin's and Runia's laments that chronological, objectivistic history is still the norm; the discipline that sees itself as concerned with change has failed to change along with the world.

This multiplicity of times does produce greater variability, and no doubt there will be unease in this heterogeneity, even relativity. But perhaps the greatest worry (apart from those who desire to maintain the mythic structure) is the loss of the synchronizing (ordering) function of chronological time. But we must remember that synchronization in our linear system is of forms and appearances that have masked the diverse human and social processes that are a part of life. We forget that people have long coordinated communication despite different times, and if we remember Whitehead's statement in the previous chapter, we already practice it. We also need to remember that the certainty is of a knowledge system (spatialized times) in which "humanity would be increasingly written out of the story of our planet" (Bowker 2005: 71).

My proposal is to overcome the difficulty by recognizing the variability of ways that a less homogeneous time can be used to achieve gradually histories that are built on multiple times. I adapt an idea, decision trees, from the Force11 scholarly communication community (see Force11 2017). The collective recognizes that the inherited mode of dissemination of scholarly research has a long history but that in today's environment, its continuation is unsupportable (financially). Many argue that it no longer fosters communication (in favor of publication), and better alternatives are already available.[13] This is not a project to eliminate corporate involvement, especially of the commercial presses; that is not possible nor necessarily desirable. A major goal is to shift scholarly work from production (publication) to communication where work flows and access have fewer legacy impediments. A major problem is the breadth, or the ecology of scholarly communication—individual practices, disciplinary and institutional cultures, and built environments. The strength of this community is its recognition that achievement of goals (varied and often disputed) requires new tools, institutional support, and—more difficult—the transformation of scholarly habits, work flows, and institutional systems—scholars, departments, libraries, publishers, foundations, and so on. The idea of decision trees recognizes that movement occurs at varying levels, depending on a variety of conditions. The decision trees help practitioners—newcomers and experienced—understand the different ways that they may participate, even though not yet at the ideal.

Below, I will suggest different levels by which we can move toward histories (and historical thinking) that are aware of the multiple times within which we operate and of how people might put this understanding into practice. There is a limitation to the metaphor of trees; it is directional. Decision trees include feedback but do not easily include interactions among the differing outcomes—in von Foerster's words, nontrivial change. I hope, though, that as my discussion proceeds, the possibility of interactions and of complexity becomes apparent.

Serres has used several metaphors—turbulent, crumpled, tattered—to imagine heterogeneous times. Turbulence makes it easier to visualize multiple temporalities where the linear flow of modern society is still strong, if not dominant. He writes, "Time does not always flow according to a line . . . nor according to a plan but, rather, according to an extraordinarily complex mixture, as though it reflected stopping points, ruptures, deep wells, chimneys of thunderous acceleration, rendings, gaps—all sown at random, at least in a visible disorder" (Serres with Latour 1995: 57). Turbulence allows for the flow of classical time (still the basis of our liberal-capitalist world), multiple layered times and temporalities (speeds and scales), and nonlinearity (iteration, recursion, and feedback). The images of time as a crumpled handkerchief and as tattered will help extend the notion of turbulence, the heterogeneity, disturbances to the system, the complex convergences, and relationality. The multiple metaphors are not an indication of confusion or a lack of consistency; instead, they suggest the multiple and complex ways that times coexist, are coincidental, conjoin, or interact. Crumpled time questions the efficacy of absolute time and absolute space to our understanding of pasts. In this time, time and space are mutable, not absolute. Tattered times returns us to the multiple times of each unit, and from these units, we can, along the lines of complex systems, discern the complex from collections of smaller components. Together, I hope that these metaphors help us imagine how heterogeneous times can be discussed as interacting in a heterogeneous world; they provide various ways to reconceive of history without chronology.

Layers of Time: Toward Turbulence

The first step in using this metaphor is to recognize the laminarity of flow, the layers of multiple time scales. The recognition of different time scales is an important step in historicizing our practice. Again, this is not new. In chapter 3, I discussed Braudel's three temporal scales—geographical, social, and individual man—and Koselleck's three layers: transcendent structures, repetitive structures, and singularities. We can also see the depiction of layers of timelines in Rosenberg and Grafton's *Cartographies of Time*, and Marx recognized the importance of different temporalities as well as their layered coexistence (Tomba 2013: 159–86). More recently work on biology and on the environment has led to several proposals. John H. Holland, one of the early proponents of complex adaptive systems, extrapolates from varying processes to argue for time scales that emanate from the unit of analysis: hours in the central nervous system, days in the human immune system, years in business systems, centuries in species, and millennia for our ecosystem (1995: 9–10). Each operates individually but also might interact and combine into a hierarchic system composed of interrelated subsystems that are often layered or nested. Hierarchic systems are one of the basic operating forms of complex systems. Small units following simple rules interact forming larger units, which then form larger units, and so on. The physicist Freeman Dyson has proposed six sociotemporal scales necessary for human survival: years, for that of the individual; decades, for the family; centuries, for the tribe or nation; millennia, for the culture; tens of millennia, for the species; eons, for the web of life on the planet (1992: 341–42). Stewart Brand adapted these time scales to focus on the pace and size of civilization: fashion/art, commerce, infrastructure, governance, culture, and nature (1999: 35–39).

The recognition of multiple time scales that are connected to natural—physical and biological—and social phenomena is an important step in dehistoricizing our objects of study. Change happens at different rates, depending on the particularities of the activity and unit. What one sees of these pasts (which are also of the present) is not the rise of civilization or the happenings of the nation-state but a number of different processes: the earth, cultures, societies, persons, organisms, and cells. It moves our understanding more directly toward the behavior and activity of units and toward greater variability—that is, layers of temporal systems that at different moments interact with one another.

These different time scales have coexisted throughout the existence of the earth. We are connected to all of them; they are a part of the past and present even though they have not been a part of the discipline of history. When one allows for these different time scales, the copresence of different units of analysis as well as the potential for different metrics becomes apparent. I emphasize potential because different time scales can operate within classical time. There is an important difference in these versions of multiple time scales. Holland's time scales are of different times that are generated in the activity of each unit. The others tend toward different temporalities that operate within absolute time. Both are important steps in moving away from a homogeneous time toward the multiple times that are a part of our twentieth-century understanding of time.

Layered time scales loosen the stranglehold of absolute time and absolute space as externalities and begin the movement toward multiplicities. Big History, national histories, capitalism, biographies, and stories of everyday life operate at different levels, often with different metrics. Scholars can debate the validity of these time scales (if we accept the idea of a time internal to activity, there are many more), but what becomes apparent is that our current chronological system is but one of several possibilities connected to the nation in Dyson's formula and to commerce and infrastructure in Brand's formulation. What appears as static and repetitive (unchanging) in Dyson's time scale of the individual might appear as transformation at the time scale of the tribe or nation. Placed within the long existence of the earth, our chronological system projects backward and forward from units of analysis of but one or two scales—those that emerged in concert with the industrial revolution, capitalism, and the nation-state. When considered in relation to the history of time, history and chronological time become fields of knowledge that organize pasts in support of an Anthropocene even before it was recognized as such.[14] Classical time is a metric that highlights, guides, and perpetuates a system of the recent several hundred years where prior thousands of years of happenings on the earth are its precursor and where other temporalities at the human or global levels have been folded in as states of unevenness (primitive or Orient) or without time (repetition or nature).

Layered times also have the potential to allow multiple perspectives in historical work. Each time scale places emphasis on a particular unit. In Holland, it might be the central nervous system, the human immune system, business systems, species, and ecosystems. For example, Patrick Anderson's *Autobiography of a Disease* (2017) shifts the perspective of a disease and its treatment from the patient, medical provider, or medical science to the microbe and the immune system. By recognizing the Anthropocene as an era rather than activity buried as a part of the natural evolution of the earth, this emphasis on ecological systems is an important attempt to shift nature into an active component of history rather than the inert and static object of use and exploitation.[15] Similarly, the overlay of biographies and stories has become a way to recenter the past around how individuals think and act. In each case, perspective is based on the activity of the time scale. Our current system based on classical time remains a part of the narrative, but it is decentered as one of several systems with which other time scales occasionally interact.

Historians need to be attentive to multiple time scales; we have long operated amid layered temporalities that have been subsumed into classical time.[16] This use of layered temporality begins to bring out the potential of multiple, coeval times. When we do, we might achieve what Braudel proposed decades ago and Koselleck suggested more recently. The next step toward Serres's notion of turbulence is to unpack absolute time itself.

Crumpled Times

Serres's crumpled time helps us think of relationality (as opposed to classification or order) among different units. In this metaphor, he suggests visualizing time using a handkerchief. When flat, it is geometric and one can mark things onto a two dimensional grid; we recreate the mechanical regularity of classical science. But when crumpled or torn—turbulence from interaction or external forces—time and space are mutable; distance, perspective, and relationships change. On the one hand, time is no longer a fixed metric suitable to measure similarity (closeness) or difference (distance). What was temporally distant might be proximate or vice versa.[17] Second, the various spatialized times—categories, classifications, and nations—lose their homogenizing status. Variations within those units become more pronounced and might alter the units themselves. The significance of this metaphor of crumpled time is to deny absolute time and absolute space a position external to activity. Time in this case, now times, is inherent to the activity itself—for example, through communities of practice. Through this notion of crumpled time, the separation of past from present as prior and different is no longer predetermined; we need to find other ways to understand relations, connections, and interaction. Pasts are no longer pasts (as prior and different); categories and spaces are heuristic assemblages; and things that were described as static might operate at a different time, where events distanced by dates might share many qualities.

With this understanding of crumpled times, we can expose how a "neophilia" operates to veil the gesture of exclusion. The historian of science David Edgerton points to a constancy of technological hype: "History reveals that technological futurism is largely unchanging over time" (2007: xvi). In the field of media archeology, several scholars have shown that the social application and utility of many "new" technological discoveries are similar to much earlier discoveries (Gitelman 2006; Kittler 1990; Huhtamo and Parikka 2011). Siegfried Zielinski (2006) explores the possibilities of "deep time," times where there is potential to understand beyond current categories. He looks for intersections of magic, technology, and culture to learn new things from the chronologically old. Jussi Parikka demonstrates how the Anthropocene can be more than a reconfigured era (spatialized time). The "obscene" in the title of his *Anthrobscene* is the recognition of entropy—waste, decay, and pollution—as a part of the process of production.

These examples show the possibility of times that move beyond the technological "new." They recognize that chronology fosters a technical or technological variation (improvement) over a past, the "old." Moreover, they question such linearity as change; instead, the new serves as a form of function optimization, a form of enhancement of the current, or what David Levy calls "more, better, faster" (Levy 2007). This function optimization might be change on Brand's scale of commerce, but it is the homeostasis of capitalist production on the scale of governance masqueraded through an ideology of progress, as if it is "new." Multiple times, not just scales, coexist within the same process. Edgerton has pointed out, "Calling for innovation is, paradoxically, a common way of avoiding change when change is not wanted" (2007: 210). For example, according to a Google Ngram on the word *innovation*, we see its increasing popularity from approximately 1950. Yet this is inversely related to Robert Gordon's study in which he finds that the major innovations of US society occurred between 1870 and

1970. In short, we are quite possibly using the word *innovation* more even as we are innovating less.[18]

Chronological time has led us to presume difference, even progress, and it has obscured the regularity of liberal-capitalist systems. William Sewell (2008: 519), for example, compares the tulip bubble of 1635–36 with the dot-com bubble at the beginning of the twenty-first century. He writes, "This suggests that in spite of the birth and death of firms and industries, the transformations in technology, the development of ever more sophisticated financial instruments, the greatly increased capacity of states and repeated shifts in economic policy regimes, there is some central mechanism of capitalism that has remained essentially unchanged for a century and a half" (520).[19] This repetition echoes Fukuzawa's worry of Japan's past, but now it is an indictment of our own notion of progress. Gary Fields has written a powerful study on the similarity of use of enclosure for governance in twenty-first-century Palestine, seventeenth-century England, and eighteenth-century New England. As in Sewell's example, differences, change, and progress are marked through classical time. But chronological distance and geocultural difference obscure the similarity, the "ongoing reconstitution" of the fundamental relationship of power—the repetitive process that maintains a certain economic or political power structure. These examples might be closer to the duration of the Troubles described by White than we have thought; I am reminded of Bergson, who argues that time obscures duration. They reinforce Wagner's separation of epistemic and economic progress for a few and the perpetuation of hegemony socially and politically; they support Bastian's fatal confusion where temporalities are changing differentially in unexpected ways—nature is moving faster than institutions.

In this regard, we must wonder today whether the fascination with innovation is less about change, the "new," than a condition that perpetuates the technological aspects of modern society; Innis complained about a bias toward present-mindedness in 1951, more than a half century ago (1951: 75–83). Accelerating time, especially the increase of a presentist perspective, is now a common refrain. Perhaps we are nearing an end of this era of inflationary media—the separation of object from representation—begun with the telegraph. In the first era of print, the copy sufficed for materiality. With digital media, this materiality becomes imaginary. My argument fits with Huhtamo and Parikka's *Media Archaeology* that this presentism is not a change caused by technology. Digital media are certainly related and exacerbate the condition. Instead, there seems to be an extension of the linear structure of time that has obscured its perpetuation through a reliance on sociocultural "stability." Technological improvements, efficiencies, and replacements are described as a form of change. But improvement of what? It is the improvement of a process of production and consumption that enhances and strengthens the current system.

I don't deny the possibility of change or the desire for innovation; I do, though, believe that these words are overused to the extent that, without greater specificity and understanding of times, they lose meaning and, worse, mask the repetitive process. Nowotny suggests that we don't understand the process. She writes, "The linear model of innovation . . . has been discarded, but innovation remains a process which, despite or because of its tight links to policy, is relatively little understood. As of today, there is no theory of innovation" (2016: 106). In the examples above, we see linearity when we begin with ourselves as the modern endpoint within our own time. But when examined in other times, the perspective changes. Following Wagner, we cannot deny epistemic-economic (including technological) progress, but if we use a metric of society, we raise questions about the direction of change. In 1992, Francisco Varela discerned a bias in cognitive science: the emphasis of abstract units of knowledge over units that are concrete, embodied, and lived and that form the basis for those abstractions. He continued that one of those abstractions is development (or, in history, progress) but suggests the valuation of cognitive development should be inverted: "It became apparent that the deeper and more fundamental kind of intelligence is that of a baby who can acquire language from dispersed daily utterances, or can constitute meaningful objects from a previously unspecified world" (Varela 1992: 98). If making sense of diffuse activity is the metric that demonstrates creativity or complex thinking over acquisition of information, then adults don't fare as well.

This returns us to a fundamental issue for history and nonmodern places. If we extend Varela's observation to the premodern periods or nonmodern societies and replace baby/adult with social units such as medieval/modern, Orient/Occident, or East/West, the inversion of placing the former after (i.e., superior to) the latter might strike readers as absurd. The reverse has been common—medieval culture and the Orient have frequently been described as childlike, the "not-yet." But without the gesture of exclusion that uses the past to validate the modern through measurables like power, wealth, and the military, twentieth-century history looks different. It does not automatically elevate the "not-yet" but allows for other representations.

My point is not to criticize or debunk. Instead, I hope that when freed from the limitations of chronology and modern categories, history and historical understanding will broaden and become richer. One of my suggestions throughout this work is the possibility of isomorphisms between the pre- or nonmodern and the digital; in this case, it becomes possible that our modern system is the anomaly rather than the norm. Saussy (2016) has argued that oral literatures have their own rhythms and ways of communicating; they should not be considered as prior and less accurate forms than written modes, especially since they bear many similarities to recent forms of text messaging. Foley (2012) argues in his "Pathways Project" that there is much in common between oral forms of transmission and the new electronic forms.[20] The similarities between oral and electronic forms are the networks of transmission and interaction, the openness and the sharing/remixing of material, the malleability of stories within rule-governed patterns, the contingencies of outcome, and the distributed forms of authorship.

Finally, crumpled time also calls into question the categories and spatialized times through which we have ordered modern society. We must remember that in the Enlightenment, the rise of statistics, probability, and history changed subjects from individuals to aggregates of populations. This move toward aggregates was accompanied by the breakup of time into eras (spatialized time), the fragmentation of places into nation-states, and the rise or "discovery" of the social. Classification facilitates knowing, predictability, order, and control; these are tools of maintenance and stability, not change. Serres points out the limitations of classification: "Once more, the same thing can be said again where science is concerned. The more classification there is, the less evolution there is, the more classes there are, the less history there is, the more coded sciences there are, the less invention and knowledge there are, the more administrating there is, the less movement there is" (1995: 94). My point is not to invert the order but to examine the nature of the processes by which stasis and mobility occur.

Edmund Russell (2011) shows how an understanding of heterogeneity within a category alters historical understanding. He argues that the industrial revolution became possible because of the rise of a long-fiber cotton in the New World. Cotton differed. By treating all cotton as the same, previous accounts emphasized the genius of man's invention of machinery. Russell shows, however, that cotton threads from the Old World were shorter and not strong enough for mechanization. Instead, he draws on layered times and crumpled time to offer a different explanation for the industrial revolution: the many-thousand-year process of domestication of New World cotton (*Gossypium hirsutum*) by the Native Americans; the slave-trade route that brought New World cotton to Liverpool; and the technological development of machines—spinning jenny, water frame, and mule—around Lancashire. In other words, many processes were involved in the lead-up to the mechanization of the cotton industry. For my argument, the two key issues were the multiple processes—indeed, the circularity of the technological development—and the importance of the specificity of cotton.

This brings us back to the difference between mechanical time and biological times. We have created a system of always working against organic processes—not unlike our tendency to ignore entropy (remember the warning of Sir Arthur Eddington?). The former moves toward homogeneity; the latter moves toward disorder. Classifications—spatialized time—serve as important heuristic devices. Yet they are a part of a system that trumpets uniformity and sameness while "the common rhythms of life, produce not so much uniformity as variety" (Michael Young 1988: 39). Diversity is a key to change; homogeneity is biased toward continuity. In evolution, morphogenesis often comes from variation in species that adapted in some way to changing or external conditions. Wagner argues that social progress (as "the increase in the human capacity to live life as one wants to live it"), when it has occurred, has been the result of struggle, especially from the margins (2016: 70). The computer scientist Gary Flake describes the importance of diversity in the following way: the fit agents "have little to gain and much to lose from large mutations." In contrast, the unfit agents, those on the margins, "are better served by attempting large probes, for in times of trouble, big changes are needed. If the change makes things worse, well, things were bad already" (1998: 421). Scott Page (2008), a scientist of complex systems, has conducted research that shows that diverse groups of individuals are often able to problem solve better than a group of like-minded experts. Heterogeneity is more than a question of diverse groups of individuals; it is central in fostering change, or the more trendy word today, *innovation*.

Tattered Times

The last metaphor for time used by Serres that I will discuss is "tattered." Tattered times focus on the specific historicity—the concrete and lived activity—and situatedness within each unit as well as its varied goals and purpose. We must recognize that each unit has its own history and experience. Serres writes, "Basic time is a tatter, a patchwork or a mosaic, it is a distribution, through which, at times, redundancy passes. A multiplicity marks and shows some redundancy, it becomes spatial when this repetition increases" (1995: 116). With this metaphor, we invert the relation between part and whole. The diversity of many units and their combination into larger units (the mosaic) is emphasized, not the units as a part of the whole. This time offers us a conceptual framework for finer-grain analyses that allow the heterogeneity of pasts so we can pay attention to the specificity of an activity and of the interaction between the different components prior to the codification of practices and places. In this activity and interaction, there are multiple times, various flows, and disturbances of turbulence. The whole is affected by this complex confluence. Emergence depends on the specific combination, inherited knowledge, and environment. As each participant adjusts, there is a change of quality. This process recurs. The iterative process that recognizes the change to actant and actor in every interaction approaches the nontrivial change that von Foerster differentiates. Interestingly, it places history as a part of the process as well as the post hoc recounting of actions. The potential for history is to become less a narrative of particular places and events than a recounting of ways that people move, how objects and things are formed from repetitive patterns, and the emergence of "permanences."

Tim Ingold's notion of a "taskscape," the pattern of dwelling activities, provides an example of an internal time that emerges from activity (1993: 153).[21] He describes it as "a total movement of becoming which builds itself into the forms we see, and in which each form takes shape in continuous relation to those around it" (164). Ingold then continues, encapsulating the significance of the taskscape: "The world itself takes on the character of an organism" (164). Ingold brings out the relevance of organic processes over mechanical time. The difference can be illustrated through two rather similar descriptions that are based on very different understandings of time and motion or of duration and mobility. In his critique of history, Jacques Rancière describes its basic framework as development and progress that go "from the simplest activities to the most complex systems of activity" (1994: 80). Melanie Mitchell describes the goal of complex systems as "to explain how complex behavior can arise from large collections of simpler components" (2009: x). The words are similar but the difference is in *to* and *from*. Simple to complex is linear: repetitive to progressive, backward to advanced, slowest to liveliest, and so on. This corresponds to time and motion. Complex from simple is based on the activity of basic units that coalesce into increasingly complex systems; this corresponds to duration and mobility.

Crucially, redundancy (repetition) is not the characteristic of an originary state but the action that leads to more and more complex systems. Repetition often gives rise to place. It slows down time; it is the spatialization of time. Change also emerges from repetition; repetitive acts do not repeat exactly. The changes might be small, but in each iteration, the environment, conditions, and understandings all differ. After several iterations, variation (change) becomes more noticeable. These times can be that of some organic system: a pathogen, flea, dog, plant, human, ecosystem, and so on. This is one place where the interaction of diverse agents—of the same or different times—brings about nontrivial change. Hannah Landecker (2016) shows the potential—indeed, the necessity— for analyses that recognize different times in her essay on drug resistance. As antibiotics, such as penicillin, seemed to work like "miracle" drugs, other processes were also continuing—pathogens were also changing. She calls the former a history of biology and the latter a biology of history. At the same time that labs were engineering new bacterial genomes to cure diseases, there is another story of growing resistance where plasmids (carriers used to move DNA) move horizontally to more than the targeted bacteria, often transferring resistance. It is an iterative, evolving, and coconstituting process. Bertalanffy writes, "The organism is not a static system closed to the outside and always containing the identical components; it is an open system in a (quasi-)steady state, maintained constant in its mass relations in a continuous change of component material and energies, in which material continually enters from, and leaves into, the outside environment" (1968: 121). If we focus on these times that are based on organisms (of which humans and society are a part), our notion of change becomes much more varied and richer. We must consider growth, decay, different rates, durative times, homeostasis, repetition, recursion, feedback, and so on.

One place of potential for historical understanding is to open the possibility of histories that move away from a structure that is biased toward the mechanical and measurable. Above all, this emphasis on the activity of organisms and communities of practice inverts the role of temporalities—such as repetition—in our understanding of humans and societies; a focus on activity and practice decenters units and categories as default subjects and opens inquiry to experience and life. This is the power of Varela's statement; he questions whether the categories we have internalized are valid— the more one knows, the more advanced he or she is (maybe or maybe not true—this is especially relevant for academia, where the internet places information at the fingertips of many).

Scholars have long recognized repetition as a problematic condition within modern society. In 1893, Emile Durkheim wrote, "Civilisation has imposed upon man monotonous and continuous labor, which implies an absolute regularity in habits" (Michael Young 1988: 73). Anson Rabinbach (1990) has written a fine study that shows the rise of disease (neurasthenia) during the late nineteenth century related to increasing speed and repetitive motion. Robert Musil muses over the decline of human sensibility in the face of mechanistic processes of modern society. He writes, "What has arisen is a world of qualities without a man, of experiences without someone to experience them. ... Probably the dissolution of the anthropocentric way of relating ... has finally made its way to the self. What one still calls personal destiny today is threatened by collective and ultimately statistically comprehensible processes" (quoted in Luft 1980: 217). Elizabeth Goodstein points out that boredom is a modern concept that is tied to progress and clock time (2005: 1–7). This acceleration of repetition arose around the same time that Ranke turned to the archives to write (and transform) history. As history was becoming institutionalized, common people were increasingly subject to mechanical and progressive time, but it was in the mechanical repetition of factory work and everyday life. Goodstein calls this boredom "experience without qualities," and we can connect these accounts to recent comments on the increasing speed and banality of life. I am sympathetic to these critiques, yet they operate through mechanical, classical time. Repetition is treated as a malady—banality, boredom, or anomie. It is a living death. But too often, this has been an ideological panacea that has locked people into the system they are trying to move beyond. Kant recognized this problem, but advocates deferred gratification: "To feel one's life, to enjoy oneself, is nothing other than to feel oneself continually driven to go beyond the present state" (quoted in Goodstein 2005: 90–91). The difficulty, if not the futility, of this remedy is increasingly apparent today.

But this focus on activity has the potential to bring back repetition as a form of stability, a desired human sensibility that modern history has deemphasized, even denigrated. Georg Simmel offers a provocative interpretation that suggests a more organic basis of time. It turns our focus toward the human first rather than the categories and institutions of modernity. He writes, "The deepest problems of modern life flow from the attempt of the individual to maintain the independence and individuality of his existence against the sovereign powers of society, against the weight of the historical heritage and the external culture and technique of life" (Simmel [1903] 2002: 11). Simmel is concerned with individuals, but we can also think of other scales of social units—communities, objects, ideas, kingdoms, and nation-states. Similarly, the sciences of cybernetics and GST also moved beyond the mechanical causality of classical science and looked for behavior and process. Bertalanffy writes, "Experienced time is not Newtonian. . . . It depends on physiological conditions" (1968: 230).

Experience and relations exist independent of, in interaction with, and against pasts that are of the present—heritage, external culture, and techniques of life. We must pay attention to people who, although within the nation-state, do not always subscribe to its conditions. Serres, echoing Simmel, describes the absence of history from his childhood home: "I knew and still know places and people who exist without history." They did not participate in it, did not seek to understand it, were uninterested, and when they encountered it (conscription), they hated it (Serres with Latour 1995: 19). This distrust or disinterest in history is evident in Harootunian's description of his parents' forgetting of and disinterest in the Armenian Genocide in their new lives in the US (2017). For the decades following World War II, few Japanese Americans discussed the concentration camps.[22] Indrani Chatterjee (2013) focuses on the "forgotten" peoples of Northeast India through the activities of monastic orders, the administrative, social, and economic center of the lives of inhabitants. This community, though, is gradually written out of history—first by the British colonizers, who described the people as savage and the community as tribal, and second by postcolonial historians, who repeated the categories. Sanja Perovic (2017) has examined the Peterlee Project of Stuart Brisley, a public history project to establish a history of a new community created by displacing people from their mining past. The relevance here is the blockage by community members themselves against the critical (liberal) ideals of Brisley himself. Each operated in different times.

One can see in each of these cases how heterogeneous pasts exist in different times and how those activities might conjoin at particular moments.[23] Each operates according to its own time; the cases are trying to maintain their own dynamic equilibrium yet encounter turbulence when a linear history shows its agential desires and tries to colonize them (through help, advice, incorporation, or violence) if they allow it. That is their separation from history. These histories are heterogeneous and operate through their own internal time. They bring out a tension with the multiple times and temporalities and what Fraser identifies as the time-compact order, the homogenizing tendency of history.

BEGINNINGS, AGAIN

In arguing for the histories that reflect the multiple times in our worlds, I am not arguing for another or "new" narrative style that should replace our current system. To do so might lead to a subsumption that reduces heterogeneity into a new homogenizing structure. I am advocating for multiples where chronological time is decentered to but one of many times (currently the dominant one). Without the metric of chronology, we (historians) have the opportunity to think anew about change and order—that is, to open up to Bergson's "true reality" (quoted in the epigraph). I agree with Marc Bloch that "history is the science of people in time" (1953: 27) but modify it to the multiple times now common in the sciences. History then becomes a science[24] in heterogeneous times—repetition, layered time scales, circular causality, and nonlinear processes—that are inherent to the activity of systems. These multiple times coexist; they might be independent, and at different points, they interact, coincide, conjoin, or collide. From this activity, interaction, repetition, or recurrence give rise to patterns and commonality—the spatialization of time. Change can be maintenance (homeostasis), decay, innovation, and/or growth. Events separated by chronological time might not be that different while rates of activity vary: viruses multiply very quickly, society moves rather slowly, geological masses move even more slowly, and today, the environment seems to be moving faster than the latter two.

When we recognize these multiple times, historical change becomes much more than measurable movement in chronological time. Change is in the activity, interaction, and outcome of one thing in connection with others, each with their own time and operating at different rates. The particular environment matters, and history is also actant, as a filter of what one sees, of how one understands, and of what one ignores. Perspective, heterogeneity, and multiplicity are assumed, and relationality and situatedness become fundamental conditions. This is certainly more complex than linear causal narratives, but it is increasingly apparent that our current system is out of sync. Almost fifty years ago, Ernst Bloch (1970) used the work based on the nineteenth-century mathematician Bernhard Riemann for a flexible time and space to conceptualize our world in his *A Philosophy of the Future*. He wrote, "The firmer the refusal of a purely Western emphasis, and of one laid solely upon development to date (to say nothing of discredited imperialism), all the stronger is the help afforded by a utopian, open and in itself still experimental orientation. Only thus can hundreds of cultures flow into the unity of the human race; a unity that only then takes shape, in non-linear historical time, and with an historical direction that is not fixed and monodic" (140–41). I believe multiple times is closer to Bergson's "true reality."

CODA

My working hypothesis is that all views of history have been fundamentally shaped by the way records are duplicated, knowledge transmitted, and information stored and retrieved.

—Elizabeth Eisenstein (1966: 40)

Now is the time to imagine how we will reconstruct our memory systems to accommodate abundance.

—Abby Smith Rumsey (2016: 136)

This work began with what I thought would be a fun, short digital essay—I now know that there is no such thing as a short digital project. That original work is still unpublished, and I will turn back to it soon—hopefully it will be a digital example of a history without chronology. It has pushed me to first principles, an inquiry into chronological time in historical thinking, and elsewhere explorations into new practices of scholarly communication. The most worrisome aspect has been the ways that digital media, especially the way that information is dynamic—how it is created, duplicated, stored, and disseminated—is transforming the conditions on which we know and decide.[1] This is Eisenstein's important hypothesis. Historians—indeed, all scholars whose work touches pasts—certainly need to attend to these processes that affect "all views of history." Whether we agree or not, we should all pause when reading Mayer-Schönberger's simple but disturbing statement: "Digital remembering erodes time" (2009: 113). It certainly erodes chronological time. There are other times that, I believe, operate and can help us comprehend these changes.

When we understand that history and time have their own histories, we also see that those histories are also situated in a complex ecology, with various actors seeking to adapt, forestall, combine, understand, or embrace the myriad events. This relation between information inflation and society has a long history. We can see this as the interplay between new artifices of recording (back to Socrates) to today's anxiety about how recording technologies change cognition and sociality.[2] The history we practice today is a part of earlier work to order and control a world of expanded information; it has been about taxonomies and hierarchies that unify diversity into a predictable system. In the process of creating that system, it inverted the way people know and understand their surroundings. In history, it has become about the past of collective units—places and people—using the filtered information—that is, the facts that support those narratives. Chronology has been a key metric in this structure of order and control.

From her perspective in the computer sciences, Melanie Mitchell describes the limitations of our current knowledge system based on Newtonian time and space: "Many phenomena have stymied the reductionist program: the seemingly irreducible unpredictability of weather and climate; the intricacies and adaptive nature of living organisms and the diseases that threaten them; the economic, political, and cultural behavior of societies; the growth and effects of modern technology and communications networks; and the nature of intelligence and the prospect for creating it in computers" (2009: x). This covers most of the sciences, social sciences, and humanities! We operate in a system that is increasingly unsuitable as a framework for understanding our world; our knowledge system is desynchronized from the structures it helps stabilize. On top of this, today digital media are destabilizing inherited institutions and concepts through the exponential growth of information.

This is a good moment (indeed, now more important than ever), as Abby Smith Rumsey suggests in the epigraph, to imagine our relation with pasts. It is an important moment, a famous intellectual argues, to consider "the ways we operate for whom our past, history, or traditions are part of our makeup" (quoted in Kleinberg 2017: 5). Few historians, I believe, would disagree with this statement. For me, it suggests the need to invert, again, our understanding of where we begin from mobility as opposed to masses that move and see stability as an outcome, not some originary state.[3] This shifts the basis of our knowledge from Newtonian time to times of organic processes. This then leads us to embrace the heterogeneity of the globe and also to emphasize relationality; it is grounded in the science of the twentieth century (and hopefully beyond), not that of the seventeenth century. The famous intellectual quoted above is Jacques Derrida. He suggests this inversion, a different engagement with pasts. They are not the dead archives but a constantly changing arena that is also a part of the present, varies as things come and go, and has multiple meanings and perspectives; history is more than a narrative of becoming something that was "real." Tradition can be the inherited knowledge, understanding, and practices that also filter what people know and believe. For scholars who criticize Enlightenment-based knowledge, the past has always been mutable. Today, pasts are dynamic. Regardless of whether pasts are dead, mutable, or dynamic, these changes indicate more attention is needed on the use, function, and content of those pasts. This certainly challenges if not changes "all views of history."

I believe that the past (or, more accurately, pasts) is and remains crucial. If we weaken pasts (and histories), we risk moving toward Fraser's fear, a time-compact order. We need to maintain pasts, but pasts should not be juxtaposed to the new. Instead, they should be connected to various features of society. History is decreasingly able to maintain the aura of solidity that has characterized our liberal-capitalist societies as well as the international one since the nineteenth century. Above all, we need to be wary of the various categories that we thought were natural or common sense.[4]

To begin parsing these distinctions, we must embrace and also be cautious of digital technologies. Digital media can be disruptive; digital technologies can reinforce the status quo. Today, they are doing both. As digital media are changing the basis of information, digital technologies are also tools that facilitate the management (or aura of containment) of the ever-increasing information. For example, using digital archives, database technology, word processing, and social media offers the illusion of being at the forefront (of digital humanities, Big Data, etc.). Some tools are. But more commonly they offer the way to do more, be faster, and find better information. This process of innovation reinforces the existing system. The idea of being "cutting edge" (temporally measured) or more advanced masks a repetition, a maintenance of a practice. For example, it supports the treadmill of academic production.[5] I agree with critics who see most digital humanities projects as porting analog systems and concepts to digital technologies; it becomes a digital variation of a discipline (history) that seeks order and control of information.[6] But this is a reason to seriously engage, not to avoid it. This is the excitement of our uncertain system; the opportunity, as Smith Rumsey asserts in the epigraph, to "imagine how we will reconstruct our memory systems."

I hope that this argument to decenter chronology provides provocations to explore the rich diversity of pasts and presents that history has tended to subsume. The recognition that our current understanding fixes relational understanding and then masks it through system and ideology of progressive motion is central to understanding history; it also guiles us to accept technological advancements as an overall improvement while maintaining the status quo. I find this recognition intellectually liberating; it has opened doors to similar concerns in different fields, to new questions, to formerly discarded pasts, and to other ways to make connections among pasts and of pasts with the present. It also provides linkages and openings—the situatedness of evidence, the variability of reading and learning, the multiplicity of times, the relationality of interactions, and a reconsideration of change—that connect to the disruptions of digital media. History can be more and more important than it currently allows itself to be.

We will not know where we will end up—whether we are facing a breakdown of our existing system, whether we are in transition, or whether we have already entered some new understanding—until it has passed. Though I did not set out in this direction, this book joins more and more research in a wide range of fields that is questioning whether our current knowledge system, post-Enlightenment, is an anomaly, not the norm or the most advanced. It is hard to resist the similarity with Certeau's description of the world that the church had dominated. Certeau describes the effort of mystics: "They intended to *reorganize places for people to communicate* in the aftermath of the breakdown of a system that until then had implemented relation through a hierarchized and cosmological network combining ontological states (lineage, truth values) with stable alliances (social clienteles, or contracts between words and things)" (1992: 165). In our world today, chronological time creates the hierarchy, science is the cosmology, and liberal-capitalism inserts stable alliances into the ontological state. Opening up history as a place for discussing relations and meaning strikes me as a good endeavor.

THE PASTS THEY ARE A-CHANGIN'[7]

The word and concept of *information* is today ubiquitous. We hear much about the "information revolution," whatever that is. It certainly appears as an inundation; information, databases, and algorithms are more and more ubiquitous. Big Data, the emerging field to manage this inflation, is hot (or the latest panacea). Yet there are similarities between this current moment of information inflation and the previous one, from which modern history emerged. Historians have long dealt with information as facts and documents; algorithms too are meant to order, manage, and control more and more data. Both make claims to objectivity or neutrality, but an important variation is that even though, as I have argued, situatedness makes documents and the "facts" less stable; electronic media makes even the facade of that stability less tenable. Data and information today are dynamic. Documents are produced, transmitted, reproduced, stored, and read electronically. Furthermore, at each step, there are electronic mediations that are also dynamic. There is no materiality to fall back on to claim originality, authenticity, reality, and so on (Ernst 2002: 115). More than ever, this calls for a need to examine the situatedness that gives rise to facts or data as well as their varied meanings that depend on perspective.

In our digital age, the idea of the historian as an expert who can recount facts of a particular time and space is a futile endeavor in the face of the internet, with its growing and near instantaneous ability for recall. Yet the role of historians—of historical knowledge, I believe—becomes more important. The folklorist John Miles Foley exhorts, "Put aside the expectations that arise from the ideology of texts—that knowledge, art, and ideas can be converted to finite, fixed things—and embrace the truth that you are negotiating and co-creating through exploring pathways" (2012: 74). What Foley calls the pathways—the meanings, semiotics, interpretations, and perspectives that are usually ignored in the cybernetic sciences (what has been attributed to Claude Shannon's category of "noise" in his classic essay [Shannon and Weaver 1949])—speaks to a methodological strength of historians and humanists to understand the surroundings, embeddedness, situatedness, and environment. It is important to remember Droysen's statement, "Facts are stupid without interpretation," which would make a terrific meme if *facts* were changed to "Data are stupid without interpretation." Like the mystics described by Certeau, historians, by moving beyond the context to situatedness, can be well equipped to "reorganize places for people to communicate."

A shift from chronological time to multiple times began this inquiry. History is not just description of the past. History and pasts are also actants, filters that people use to understand situations; they become a constituent condition of any interaction. Events are interpreted (and altered) several times—by the witness (or witnesses), by the historian, and by the reader/audience. Perspective necessarily shifts from the monocular to the multiple. Interestingly, this recalls the controversial essays by Jordan (2018) and Marcus (2018) that point to the limitations of decontextualized data in the deep learning subfield of artificial intelligence. Repetition seems to also be a part of our current knowledge system. There seems to be a parallel to the creation of Ranke's paper archive in the 1830s to the digital archive today. Information is shorn of the milieu that gave the data meaning, even existence, in the first place. This abstraction of data recalls the bracketing of issues of meaning and human variability at the Macy Conferences.[8]

This is not a "mere" appeal for the humanities; it is hard to imagine a society that remembers everything and cannot interpret (or forget) its data. I must modify my statement that the past is important: it is important, but not all pasts need be remembered. Alexander Luria (1987) documented such a person in his classic book *The Mind of a Mnemonist*. S. remembered everything. Long-term planning was impossible; he was always in the present (the past is still remembered and active). Yet we have become a society that seemingly records everything (Mayer-Schönberger 2009). I see the concerns about presentism or extended present as consistent with our twentieth-century understanding of time. Hartmut Rosa (2003) suggests that this presentism is a logical outcome of our system of constant forward movement—he calls it acceleration.

In his introduction to the transcripts of the Macy Conferences, Claus Pias suggests that while cybernetics has brought a multilinear understanding of times, especially through feedback and homeostasis, it has also perhaps helped shorten our horizon into the future. He writes, "It suddenly seemed conceivable . . . to program 'conscious human targets' that, so long as the appropriately oriented mechanisms of communication and control are in place, would always already have been met. The tense of cybernetics would thus be something like the future perfect: Everything will have been" (2016: 20–21). Pias describes how research in datacentric fields (like Big Data) is concerned about predicting behavior. Fields such as artificial intelligence, computer science, and robotics depend on models (from some past behavior), which machines use to predict what will happen—for example, weapons targeting, self-driving cars, and social media. (The field of targeted advertising adds new meaning to "conscious human targets.") Extrapolation, prediction, or anticipation of some pattern or model suffices for the future. It is, again, a legacy of linear time. Peter Bexte writes, "Modern societies depend on the future like drug addicts on their dealer" (2011: 222). Today, it is data; before, it was facts. In both cases, there is an obsession with recording. I see a parallel with Benjamin's statement that "as they really were" is the narcotic of the twentieth century. These words turn to both ends of the gesture of exclusion; a certain past stabilizes what is to come. A good example is the reports from several years ago about search algorithms that were drawing from and reinforcing gender and racial stereotypes of the (one had hoped early) twentieth century (Jobin 2013; Chemaly 2015). We must recognize that history and its various methods have served as a filtering system.

My point in raising this is not to dispute the truth or falsity of these searches. Instead, they suggest the need to parse out the ideology of change, the multiple times that coexist, and the operations within which events occur. At minimum, this calls for an understanding of time that is beyond the simplistic (and mythical) notion of time as past, present, future. This linearity ignores the multiple ways that these temporalities are used to support a mechanical process; it obscures a bifurcation where (as in other structures of modern society) technology, the new, has a hand in maintaining the past. Technological innovation facilitates the future perfect "everything will have been" (Pias 2016: 21). More broadly, this repetitive system that serves a belief in technological progress is also the communicative world of social media—the perpetual present that is maintained with feedback loops (e.g., likes on social media). This relationship between prediction, anticipation, and repetition is not new. It has existed within history but has been masked as progress. Nowotny calls this the extended present. At minimum, we must also consider the contents embedded in these categories. It is necessary to question this notion of the future; anticipation, the future, and goals are not the same.

Historians can be among the most equipped scholars to understand this relationship of times and the different ways that they are used despite ideologies of innovation. It is, to repeat Derrida, to focus on "the ways we operate for whom our past, history, or traditions are part of our makeup" (quoted in Kleinberg 2017: 5). Each—the past, history, and traditions—is much broader and plays a more active role than our current history allows.

Finally, this inquiry suggests the importance of turning to recent science as well as pre-Enlightenment (and nonmodern) practices. The cybernetic turn to existing models and patterns to anticipate adjustments can be a beginning for how we think about history without chronology. Time frames must be much more extensive and variable. The past can contain realms that make histories more important by freeing them from the confines of chronological time. This past is not a dead, distant past but has ideas and practices that still have relevance today and tomorrow. On the other hand, scholars in widely divergent fields are interestingly turning to earlier forms of understanding, operating, and interacting for ways that people operated (and might operate) without the teleologies of development or the homogenizing structures. Theoretical physicist Carlo Rovelli suggests that a world without chronological time will look "in the simplest way, the same way we had thought about the world until Newton" (2018: 117). Historian Helge Jordheim (forthcoming) argues for eighteenth-century chronologies as the basis for a new history, but they are the chronologies of universal history, before the unification of time and the formulation of a world history. Andrew Shyrock and Daniel Lord Smail (2011) argue for a "deep time." The folklorist Foley (2012) argues that the oral mode of communication is more similar to the digital modes and the text-based mode is the outlier. In the field of media archaeology, many scholars, such as Siegfried Zielinski, are looking to the distant past to "find something new in the old" (2006: 3). Shorn of chronological ordering that marks events and periods as old or outmoded, these scholars are finding modes of understanding and interacting that might offer suggestions for our future. But this is not a romantic escape to a "better" time. It is searching for hints for how people and things interoperate (and how we might re-present these complex interactions). These are worlds where observers are also actants, multiple perspectives are recognized, and knowledge of the past—inherited understandings and practices—affect how people adapt. This is one of the goals of Certeau's work on mystics—history should again emphasize how people communicate.

HUMILITY

A good place to start for histories that embrace the times of the twentieth century is with humility; we must recognize the impossibility of the past century's effort to regularize and order the world into some universal system that maps, orders, and knows the world. That was the goal of the Enlightenment; it has been a system that dealt with the information inflation that began with the printing press. Newton's science provided the structure. We know it is flawed; following it brings the uncertainty suggested above by Mitchell. Perhaps a plea for humility is a bit incongruous for a study that proposes that history think differently about time, a system historians have used for two hundred years. I am not the first. Gabrielle Spiegel writes, "With all due humility, I would like to register my plea that we read medieval historical texts as cultural phenomena, by returning them to the social context in which they originated and from which they drew both form and meaning" (1997: 110). I would modify this by removing one word, *medieval*. This is an inversion where the excluded—past, foreign, Orient, and marginalized—no longer constitute but inform the modern. Without the metric of chronology, we can see similarities to earlier periods. We can learn from Nicholas de Cusa in his work *Of Learned Ignorance* ([1954] 1967). For de Cusa, human apprehension can never attain that of the divine, the Maximum. To this, we might add the belief in complete knowledge by filling in all the gaps or that we have reached the end of history. A goal of clarity and understanding is certainly desirable, but we must recognize that the impossibility of knowing is in the diversity of the world as well as the limitations of humans. For hints, we can turn to some of the sciences; Bertalanffy argued that organisms are dynamic: they are actants, not just objects, in continuous change, always interacting with material and energy even in a (quasi-) steady state. Representation and understanding shift with the relation of observer and observed. Sheila Jasanoff argues for "disciplined methods to accommodate the partiality of scientific knowledge and to act under irredeemable uncertainty" (2007: 33). We can replace the word *scientific* with the word *historical*. Jasanoff calls for "technologies of humility." When she describes these technologies, she is describing what I see as the strength, or what should be the strength, of history: those tools "compel us to reflect on the sources of ambiguity, indeterminacy and complexity" (2007: 33). This is what many historians have tried to do—to encompass such variability. Yet the structure and methods, I believe, have steered us in a different direction.[9] My emphasis on heterogeneity and revisiting change is my attempt at more than reflection, but I propose to think anew about our pasts. For those uncomfortable with this variability, it is time to understand that the quest for a singular truth is a myth of the Enlightenment. We must recall Bertalanffy (1968), who writes that objectivity is not the counter to relativity; relativity is the norm.

The immediate outcome is unclear; risk is involved. But I find that option better than following a system that has proven to be mythical and has been suitable for mechanistic rather than human organization.

Works Cited

Adam, Barbara. 1990. *Time and Social Theory*. Philadelphia: Temple University Press.

———. 1995. *Timewatch: The Social Analysis of Time*. Cambridge: Polity.

———. 2004. *Time*. Malden: Polity.

Akyeampong, Emmanuel, Caroline Arni, Pamela Kyle Crossley, Mark Hewitson, William H. Sewell Jr., participants. 2015. "AHR Conversation: Explaining Historical Change; or, The Lost History of Causes." *American Historical Review* 120, no. 4 (October): 1369–423.

Albers, Josef. (1963) 1975. *Interaction of Color*. New Haven: Yale University Press. Citations refer to revised edition.

Allen, David. 2001. *Getting Things Done: The Art of Stress-Free Productivity*. New York: Viking.

Althusser, Louis, and Étienne Balibar. 1970. *Reading Capital*. Translated by Ben Brewster. New York: Pantheon Books.

Anderson, Benedict. 1991. *Imagined Communities: Reflections on the Origin and Spread of Nationalism*. London: Verso.

Anderson, Patrick. 2017. *Autobiography of a Disease*. London: Routledge.

Ashby, W. Ross. 1956. *An Introduction to Cybernetics*. London: Methuen.

Ashton, Kevin. 2015. *How to Fly a Horse: The Secret History of Creation, Invention, and Discovery*. New York: Anchor Books.

Augustine. 1961. *Confessions*. Translated with an introduction by R. S. Pine-Coffin. New York: Penguin Books.

Bacon, Francis. (1620) 2004. *The New Organon*, edited by Lisa Jardine and Michael Silverthorne, 69. Cambridge: Cambridge University Press.

Bakker, Egbert J. 2002. "The Making of History: Herodotus' *Historiēs Apodexis*." In *Brill's Companion to Herodotus*, edited by Egbert J. Bakker, Irene J. F. De Jong, and Hans Van Wees, 3–32. Leiden: Brill.

Barak, On. 2013. *On Time: Technology and Temporality in Modern Egypt*. Berkeley: University of California Press.

Bartky, Ian R. 2000. *Selling the True Time: Nineteenth-Century Timekeeping in America*. Stanford: Stanford University Press.

Bastian, Michelle. 2012. "Fatally Confused: Telling the Time in the Midst of Ecological Crises." *Environmental Philosophy* 9, no. 1: 23–48.

Becker, Carl. 1932. "Everyman His Own Historian." *American Historical Review*. 37, no. 2: 221–36.

Benjamin, Walter. 1968a. "The Storyteller." In *Illuminations*, edited by Hannah Arendt and translated by Harry Zohn, 83–109. New York: Schocken Books.

———. 1968b. "Theses on the Philosophy of History." In *Illuminations*, edited by Hannah Arendt and translated by Harry Zohn, 253–64. New York: Schocken Books.

———. 1999. *The Arcades Project*. Translated by Howard Eiland and Kevin McLaughlin. Cambridge, MA: Belknap Press.

Bergson, Henri. (1913) 2001. *Time and Free Will: An Essay on the Immediate Data of Consciousness*. Translated by F. L. Pogson. Mineola: Dover.

———. 2002. "The Perception of Change." In *Henri Bergson: Key Writings*, edited by Keith Ansell Pearson and John Mullarkey. New York: Continuum.

Bertalanffy, Ludwig von. 1968. *General System Theory: Foundations, Development, Applications*. Revised edition, New York: George Braziller.

Bexte, Peter. 2011. "Uncertainty in Grammar / The Grammar of Uncertainty: Some Remarks on the Future Perfect." *From Science to Computational Sciences: Studies in the History of Computing and Its Influence on Today's Science*, edited by Gabriele Gramelsberger, 219–26. Zurich: diaphanes.

Birth, Kevin K. 2012. *Objects of Time: How Things Shape Temporality*. New York: Palgrave Macmillan.

Blackbourn, David, and Geoffrey Eley. 1984. *The Peculiarities of German History: Bourgeois Society and Politics in Nineteenth-Century Germany*. Oxford: Oxford University Press.

Bloch, Ernst. 1970. *A Philosophy of the Future*. Translated by John Cumming. New York: Herder and Herder.

Bloch, Marc. 1953. *The Historian's Craft*. Translated by Peter Putnam. New York: Vintage Books.

Blumenberg, Hans. 1985. *Work on Myth*. Translated by Robert M. Wallace. Cambridge, MA: MIT Press.

Boellstorff, Tom. 2007a. *A Coincidence of Desire: Anthropology, Queer Studies, Indonesia*. Durham: Duke University Press.

———. 2007b. "When Marriage Fails." *GLQ* 13, nos. 2–3: 227–48.

Bolter, Jay David, and Richard Grusin. 2000. *Remediation: Understanding New Media*. Cambridge, MA: MIT Press.

Bowker, Geoffrey. 2005. *Memory Practices in the Sciences*. Cambridge, MA: MIT Press.

———. 2014. "All Together Now: Synchronization, Speed, and the Failure of Narrative." *History and Theory* 53 (December): 563–76.

Brand, Stewart. 1999. *The Clock of the Long Now: Time and Responsibility*. New York: Basic Books.

Braudel, Fernand. 1980. "History and the Social Sciences: The *Longue Durée*." In *On History*. Translated by Sarah Matthews, 25–54. Chicago: University of Chicago Press.

Buber, Martin. 1970. *I and Thou*. Translated by Walter Kaufman. New York: Touchstone.

Carr, Nicholas. 2010. *The Shallows: What the Internet Is Doing to Our Brains*. New York: W. W. Norton.

Carlyle, Thomas. 2002. "On History." In *Historical Essays*, edited by Chris R. Vanden Bossche, 3–13. Berkeley: University of California Press.

Castellani, Brian. 2013. "Map of Complexity Science." Accessed July 1, 2017. http://scimaps.org/mapdetail/map_of_complexity_sc_154.

Castillo, David R., and William Egginton. 2017. *Medialogies: Reading Reality in the Age of Inflationary Media*. New York: Bloomsbury Academic.

Certeau, Michel de. 1984. *The Practice of Everyday Life*. Translated by Steven F. Rendall. Berkeley: University of California Press.

———. 1986. *Heterologies: Discourse on the Other*. Translated by Brian Massumi. Minneapolis: University of Minnesota Press.

———. 1988. *The Writing of History*. Translated by Tom Conley. New York: Columbia University Press.

———. 1992. *The Mystic Fable*. Vol. 1, *The Sixteenth and Seventeenth Centuries*. Translated by Michael B. Smith. Chicago: University of Chicago Press.

———. 2015. *The Mystic Fable*. Vol. 2, *The Sixteenth and Seventeenth Centuries*. Edited by Luce Giard. Translated by Michael B. Smith. Chicago: University of Chicago Press.

Chakrabarty, Dipesh. 2000. *Provincializing Europe: Postcolonial Thought and Historical Difference*. Princeton: Princeton University Press.

———. 2009. "The Climate of History: Four Theses." *Critical Inquiry* 35, no. 2: 197–222.

———. 2018. "Anthropocene Time." *History and Theory* 57, no. 1: 5–32.

Chatterjee, Indrani. 2013. *Forgotten Friends: Monks, Marriages, and Memories of Northeast India*. Oxford: Oxford University Press.

Chatterjee, Partha. 1986. *Nationalist Thought and the Colonial World: A Derivative Discourse?* Tokyo: Zed Books.

Chemaly, Soraya. 2015. "What Gender Stereotypes and Sexism Have to Do with Algorithms and Robots." *Huffington Post*, July 27, 2015. http://www .huffingtonpost.com/soraya-chemaly/what-gender-stereotypes-and-sexism -have-to-do-with-algorithms-and-robots_b_7880906.html.

Chudacoff, Howard P. 1989. *How Old Are You? Age Consciousness in American Culture*. Princeton: Princeton University Press.

Chute, Hillary L. 2016. *Disaster Drawn: Visual Witness, Comics, and Documentary Form*. Cambridge, MA: Belknap Press.

Clarke, Bruce. 2009. "Heinz von Foerster's Demons: The Emergence of Second-Order Systems Theory." In *Emergence and Embodiment: New Essays on Second-Order Systems Theory*, edited by Bruce Clarke and Mark B. N. Hansen, 34–61. Durham: Duke University Press.

———. 2014. *Neocybernetics and Narrative*. Minneapolis: University of Minnesota Press.

Clarke, Bruce, and Mark B. N. Hansen, eds. 2009. *Emergence and Embodiment: New Essays on Second-Order Systems Theory*. Durham: Duke University Press.

Cohen, Deborah, and Peter Mandler. 2015. "The History Manifesto: A Critique." *American Historical Review* 120, no. 2 (April): 530–42.

Cohen, Jeffrey J. 2003. *Medieval Identity Machines*. Minneapolis: University of Minnesota Press.

Cole, Andrew, and D. Vance Smith, eds. 2010. *The Legitimacy of the Middle Ages: On the Unwritten History of Theory*. Durham: Duke University Press.

Cole, Michael. 1985. "The Zone of Proximal Development: Where Culture and Cognition Meet." In *Culture, Communication, and Cognition: Vygotskian Perspectives*, edited by James V. Wertsch, 146–61. Cambridge: Cambridge University Press.

Collingwood, R. G. 1994. *The Idea of History*. Edited with an introduction by Jan Van Der Dussen. Revised ed., Oxford: Oxford University Press.

Connolly, William E. 2002. *Neuropolitics: Thinking, Culture, Speed*. Minneapolis: University of Minnesota Press.

Cresswell, Tim. 2006. *On the Move: Mobility in the Modern Western World*. London: Routledge.

Cronon, William. 2013. "Presidential Address: Storytelling." *American Historical Review* 118, no. 1: 1–19.

Darwin, Charles. 1877. "A Biographical Sketch of an Infant." *Mind* 2, no. 7 (July): 285–94.

Davis, Kathleen. 2010. "The Sense of an Epoch." In *Legitimacy of the Medieval Ages: On the Unwritten History of Theory*, edited by Andrew Cole and D. Vance Smith, 39–69. Durham: Duke University Press.

de Cusa, Nicholas. (1954) 1967. *Of Learned Ignorance*. Translated by Germain Heron. London: Routledge and Paul.

DeLanda, Manuel. 2006. *A New Philosophy of Society: Assemblage Theory and Social Complexity*. New York: Bloomsbury.

Dinshaw, Carolyn, Lee Edelman, Roderick A. Ferguson, Carla Freccero, Elizabeth Freeman, Judith Halberstam, Annamarie Jagose, Christopher S. Nealon, and Tan Hoang Nguyen. 2007. "Theorizing Queer Temporalities: A Roundtable Discussion." *GLQ: A Journal of Lesbian and Gay Studies* 13, nos. 2–3: 177–95.

Doxiadis, Apostolos, and Christos H. Papadimitriou. 2009. *Logicomix: An Epic Search for Truth*. New York: Bloomsbury.

Droysen, Johann Gustav. 1967. *Outline of the Principles of History*. Translated by E. Benjamin Andrews. New York: Howard Fertig.

Duguid, Paul, and John Seely Brown. 2000. *The Social Life of Information*. Boston: Harvard Business School Press.

Dupuy, Jean-Pierre. 2000. *The Mechanization of the Mind: On the Origins of Cognitive Science*. Translated by M. B. DeBevoise. Princeton: Princeton University Press.

Dyson, Freeman. 1992. "The Face of Gaia." In *From Eros to Gaia*, 338–45. New York: Pantheon.

Edgerton, David. 2007. *The Shock of the Old: Technology and Global History since 1900*. New York: Oxford University Press.

Eisenstein, Elizabeth L. 1966. "Clio and Chronos: An Essay on the Making and Breaking of History-Book Time." *History and Theory* 6:36–64.

Elias, Norbert. 1986. "Leisure in the Spare-Time Spectrum." In *Quest for Excitement: Sport and Leisure in the Civilizing Process*, edited by Norbert Elias and Eric Dunning, 91–125. New York: Basil Blackwell.

———. 1992. *Time: An Essay*. Oxford: Basil Blackwell.

Eriksen, Thomas Hylland. 2001. *Tyranny of the Moment: Fast and Slow Time in the Information Age*. London: Pluto Press.

Ermarth, Elizabeth Deeds. 1992. *Sequel to History: Postmodernism and the Crisis of Representational Time*. Princeton: Princeton University Press.

———. 2011. *History in the Discursive Condition: Reconsidering the Tools of Thought*. London: Routledge.

Ernst, Wolfgang. 2002. "Agencies of Cultural Feedback: The Infrastructure of Memory." In *Waste-Site Stories: The Recycling of Memory*, edited by Brian Neville and Johanne Villeneuve, 107–20. Albany: State University of New York Press.

Eskildsen, Kasper Risbjerg. 2008. "Leopold Ranke's Archival Turn: Location and Evidence in Modern Historiography." *Modern Intellectual History* 5, no. 3: 425–53.

Fabian, Johannes. 1983. *Time and the Other: How Anthropology Makes Its Object*. New York: Columbia University Press.

Fasolt, Constantin. 2004. *The Limits of History*. Chicago: University of Chicago Press.

Flake, Gary William. 1998. *The Computational Beauty of Nature: Computer Explorations of Fractals, Chaos, Complex Systems, and Adaptation*. Cambridge, MA: MIT Press.

Foley, John Miles. 2012. *Oral Tradition and the Internet: Pathways of the Mind*. Urbana: University of Illinois Press.

Force11. 2017. "WP3: Decision Trees." https://www.force11.org/group/scholarly -commons-working-group/wp3decision-trees.

Foucault, Michel. 1970. *The Order of Things: An Archaeology of the Human Sciences*. New York: Vintage Books.

Fraser, J. T. 1987. *Time: The Familiar Stranger*. Redmond: Tempus Books.

Frumer, Yulia. 2018. *Making Time: Astronomical Time Measurement in Tokugawa Japan*. Chicago: University of Chicago Press.

Fukuzawa Yukichi. (1874) 1973. *An Outline of a Theory of Civilization*. Translated by David Dilworth and G. Cameron Hurst. Tokyo: Sophia University Press.

Gabrys, Jennifer. 2011. *Digital Rubbish: A Natural History of Electronics*. Ann Arbor: University of Michigan Press.

Gell, Alfred. 1992. *The Anthropology of Time: Cultural Constructions of Temporal Maps and Images*. Oxford: Berg.

Geertz, Clifford. 1973. *The Interpretation of Cultures*. New York: Basic Books.

Georgescu-Roegen, Nicholas. 1986. "The Entropy Law and the Economic Process in Retrospect." *Eastern Economic Journal* 12, no. 1: 3–25.

Giard, Luce. 2015. "Introduction: Opening the Possible." In *Culture in the Plural*, by Michel de Certeau, edited by Luce Giard and translated by Tom Conley, ix–xv. Minneapolis: University of Minnesota Press.

Gieryn, Thomas F. 1999. *Cultural Boundaries of Science: Credibility on the Line*. Chicago: University of Chicago Press.

Gitelman, Lisa. 2006. *Always Already New: Media, History, and the Data of Culture*. Cambridge, MA: MIT Press.

Glennie, Paul, and Nigel Thrift. 2009. *Shaping the Day: A History of Timekeeping in England and Wales 1300–1800*. Oxford: Oxford University Press.

Goodstein, Elizabeth S. 2005. *Experience without Qualities: Boredom and Modernity*. Stanford: Stanford University Press.

Gordon, Robert J. 2016. *The Rise and Fall of American Growth: The U.S. Standard of Living since the Civil War*. Princeton: Princeton University Press.

Grafton, Antony. 1994. "The Footnote from De Thou to Ranke." *History and Theory* 33, no. 4 (December): 53–76.

Groot, Jerome de. 2009. *Consuming History: Historians and Heritage in Contemporary Popular Culture*. London: Routledge.

Gross, David. 1982. "Space, Time, and Modern Culture." *Telos* 50 (Winter): 59–78.

Guldi, Jo, and David Armitage. 2014. *The History Manifesto*. Cambridge: Cambridge University Press.

Gumbrecht, Hans Ulrich. 2003. *Production of Presence: What Meaning Cannot Convey*. Stanford: Stanford University Press.

Gurevich, Aron J. 1985. *Categories of Medieval Culture*. Translated by G. L. Campbell. Boston: Routledge and Kegan Paul.

Haber, F. C. 1975. "The Cathedral Clock and the Cosmological Clock Metaphor." In *The Study of Time II*, edited by J. T. Fraser and N. Lawrence, 399–416. New York: Springer-Verlag.

Harootunian, Harry. 2007. "Remembering the Historical Present." *Critical Inquiry* 33, no. 3 (Spring): 471–94.

———. 2015. *Marx after Marx: History and Time in the Expansion of Capitalism*. New York: Columbia University Press.

———. 2017. "Other People's History: Some Reflections on the Historian's Vocation." *Japan Forum* 29, no. 2: 139–53.

Hartog, François. 2015. *Regimes of Historicity: Presentism and Experiences of Time*. Translated by Saskia Brown. New York: Columbia University Press.

Harvey, David. 1996. *Justice, Nature, and the Geography of Difference*. Oxford: Blackwell.

Hayles, Katherine. 1999. *How We Became Posthuman: Virtual Bodies in Cybernetics, Literature, and Informatics*. Chicago: University of Chicago Press.

Hedrick, Charles W., Jr. 2006. *Ancient History: Monuments and Documents*. Malden: Blackwell.

Heims, Steve J. 1980. *John Von Neumann and Norbert Wiener: From Mathematics to the Technologies of Life and Death*. Cambridge, MA: MIT Press.

———. 1991. *The Cybernetics Group*. Cambridge, MA: MIT Press.

Herder, Johann Gottfried. 2004. *Another Philosophy of History and Selected Political Writings*. Translated with introduction and notes by Ioannis D. Evrigenis and Daniel Pellerin. Indianapolis: Hackett.

Herman, David. 2013. *Storytelling and the Sciences of Mind*. Cambridge, MA: MIT Press.

Holland, Dorothy. 1998. "Figured Worlds." In *Identity and Agency in Cultural Worlds*, edited by Dorothy Holland, William Lachicotte Jr., Debra Skinner, and Carole Cain, 49–65. Cambridge, MA: Harvard University Press.

Holland, John H. 1995. *Hidden Order: How Adaptation Builds Complexity*. New York: Basic Books.

Hölscher, Lucian. 1997. "The New Annalistic: A Sketch of a Theory of History." *History and Theory* 36, no. 3: 317–35.

Holtorf, Cornelius. 1996. "Towards a Chronology of Megaliths: Understanding Monumental Time and Cultural Memory." *Journal of European Archaeology* 4:119–53.

Huhtamo, Erkki, and Jussi Parikka, eds. 2011. *Media Archaeology: Approaches, Applications, and Implications*. Berkeley: University of California Press.

Hutchins, Edwin. 1995. *Cognition in the Wild*. Cambridge, MA: MIT Press.

Iggers, Georg G. 1968. *The German Conception of History: The National Tradition of Historical Thought from Herder to the Present*. Middletown: Wesleyan University Press.

Ingold, Timothy. 1993. "The Temporality of the Landscape." *World Archaeology* 25, no. 2: 152–74.

———. 2007. *Lines: A Brief History*. London: Routledge.

Innis, Harold. 1951. *The Bias of Communication*. Toronto: University of Toronto Press.

Irani, Lilly. 2019. *Chasing Innovation: Making Entrepreneurial Citizens in Modern India*. Princeton University Press.

Isozaki, Arata. 2006. "A Mimicry of Origin: Emperor Tenmu's Ise Jingū." In *Japanness in Architecture*, edited by David B. Stewart and translated by Sabu Kohso, 117–69. Cambridge, MA: MIT Press.

Jameson, Fred. 2003. "The End of Temporality." *Critical Inquiry* 29, no. 4 (Summer): 695–718.

Jasanoff, Sheila. 2007. "Technologies of Humility." *Nature* 450 (November): 33.

Jauss, Hans Robert. 1982. *Toward an Aesthetic of Reception*. Translated by Timothy Bahti. Minneapolis: University of Minnesota Press.

Jobin, Anna. 2013. "Google's Autocompletion: Algorithms, Stereotypes and Accountability." *Sociostrategy* (blog). Accessed July 18, 2016. http://sociostrategy .com/2013/googles-autocompletion-algorithms-stereotypes-accountability/.

Jordan, Michael I. 2018. "Artificial Intelligence—the Revolution Hasn't Happened Yet." *Medium* (April 18). https://medium.com/@mijordan3/artificial -intelligence-the-revolution-hasnt-happened-yet-5e1d5812e1e7.

Jordheim, Helge. 2012. "Against Periodization: Koselleck's Theory of Multiple Temporalities." *History and Theory* 51 (May): 151–71.

———. 2014. "Introduction: Multiple Times and the Work of Synchronization." *History and Theory* 53 (December): 498–518.

———. 2017. "Synchronizing the World as Historiographical Practice, Then and Now." *History of the Present* 7, no. 1 (Spring): 59–95.

———. Forthcoming. "Return to Chronology." *Rethinking Historical Time: New Approaches to Presentism.* Edited by Marek Tamm and Laurent Olivier. London: Bloomsbury.

Joyce, Patrick. 1999. "The Politics of the Liberal Archive." *History of the Human Sciences* 12, no. 2: 35–49.

Kahneman, Daniel. 2011. *Thinking, Fast and Slow.* New York: Farrar, Straus and Giroux.

Kennedy, Pagan. 2016. *Inventology: How We Dream Up Things That Change the World.* Boston: Houghton Mifflin Harcourt.

Kinder, Marsha. 1991. *Playing with Power in Movies, Television, and Video Games.* Berkeley: University of California Press.

Kittler, Friedrich A. 1990. *Discourse Networks 1800/1900.* Translated by Michael Metteer with Chris Cullens. Stanford: Stanford University Press.

Kleinberg, Ethan. 2017. *Haunting History: For a Deconstructive Approach to the Past.* Stanford: Stanford University Press.

Koselleck, Reinhart. 1985. *Futures Past: On the Semantics of Historical Time.* Translated by Keith Tribe. Cambridge, MA: MIT Press.

———. 2018. *Sediments of Time: On Possible Histories.* Translated and edited by Sean Franzel and Stefan-Ludwig Hoffmann. Stanford: Stanford University Press.

Kracauer, Siegfried. 1969. "Ahasuerus, or the Riddle of Time." In *History: The Last Things before the Last,* 139–63. New York: Oxford University Press.

Kuhn, Thomas S. 1977. *The Essential Tension: Selected Studies in Scientific Tradition and Change.* Chicago: University of Chicago Press.

Landecker, Hannah. 2016. "Antibiotic Resistance and the Biology of History." *Body & Society* 22, no. 4: 19–52.

Landes, David. 1983. *Revolution in Time: Clocks and the Making of the Modern World.* Cambridge, MA: Belknap Press.

Lave, Jean, and Etienne Wenger. 1991. *Situated Learning: Legitimate Peripheral Participation.* Cambridge: Cambridge University Press.

Lefebvre, Henri. 1991. *The Production of Space.* Translated by Donald Nicholson-Smith. Oxford: Blackwell.

———. 1995. "What Is Modernity." In *Introduction to Modernity,* translated by John Moore, 168–238. London: Verso.

—. 2004. *Rhythmanalysis: Space, Time and Everyday Life*. Translated by Stuart Elden and Gerald Moore. London: Continuum.

Le Goff, Jacques. 1980. "Merchant's Time and Church's Time in the Middle Ages." In *Time, Work, and Culture in the Middle Ages*, 29–42. Translated by Arthur Goldhammer. Chicago: University of Chicago Press.

—. 1988. *The Medieval Imagination*. Translated by Arthur Goldhammer. Chicago: University of Chicago Press.

—. 2015. *Must We Divide History into Periods?* Translated by Malcolm DeBevoise. New York: Columbia University Press.

Levi, Carlo. (1947) 2006. *Christ Stopped at Eboli*. New York: Farrar, Straus and Giroux.

Levinas, Emmanuel. 1969. *Totality and Infinity: An Essay on Exteriority*. Translated by Alphonso Lingis. Pittsburgh: Duquesne University Press.

Levy, David. 2007. "No Time to Think: Reflections on Information Technology and Contemplative Scholarship." *Ethics and Information Technology* 9:232–49.

Liakos, Antonis. 2017. "Historisising Twentieth-Century Historiography." *Historein* 16:139–48.

Lorenz, Chris. 2014. "Blurred Lines: History, Memory and the Experience of Time." *International Journal for History, Culture and Modernity* 2, no. 1: 43–62.

—. 2017. "'The Times They Are a-Changin'": On Time, Space and Periodization in History." *Palgrave Handbook of Research in Historical Culture and Education*. Edited by Mario Carretero, Stefan Berger, and Maria Grever, 109–31. New York: Palgrave Macmillan.

Lorenz, Chris, and Berber Bevernage, eds. 2013. *Breaking Up Time: Negotiating the Borders between Present, Past, and Future*. Göttingen: Vandenhoeck and Ruprecht.

Lores, Javier. 2009. "The Evolution of the Earth in Sixty Seconds." Produced by Claire L. Evans. YouTube video, 1:02. Uploaded February 19, 2009. www.youtube.com/watch?v=YXSEyttblMl.

Lowenthal, David. 1985. *The Past Is a Foreign Country*. Cambridge: Cambridge University Press.

Lukács, Georg. 1971. *History and Class Consciousness: Studies in Marxist Dialectics*. Translated by Rodney Livingstone. Cambridge, MA: MIT Press.

Luckmann, Thomas. 1991. "The Constitution of Human Life in Time." In *Chronotypes: The Construction of Time*, edited by John Bender and David E. Wellbery, 151–66. Stanford: Stanford University Press.

Luft, David S. 1980. *Robert Musil and the Crisis of European Culture 1880–1942*. Berkeley: University of California Press.

Luria, Alexander R. 1987. *The Mind of a Mnemonist*. Translated by Lynn Solotaroff. Cambridge, MA: Harvard University Press.

Mali, Joseph. 2003. *Mythistory: The Making of a Modern Historiography*. Chicago: University of Chicago Press.

Manovich, Lev. 2001. *The Language of New Media*. Cambridge, MA: MIT Press.

Manuel, Frank. 1963. *Isaac Newton: Historian*. Cambridge, MA: Belknap Press.

Marcus, Gary. 2018. "Deep Learning: A Critical Appraisal." arXiv:1801.00631 [cs.AI], accessed July 26, 2018.

Marx, Karl. 1900. *The Poverty of Philosophy Being a Translation of the Misère de la Philosophie*. London: Twentieth Century Press.

———. 1974. *Das Elend der Philosophie: Antwort auf Proudhoms "Philophie des Elends."* In *Werke, Band 4*, by Karl Marx and Frederick Engels, 63–124. Berlin: Dietz Verlag.

———. 1976. *The Poverty of Philosophy*. In *Collected Works*, vol. 6, *1845–1848*, by Karl Marx and Frederick Engels, 105–212. Moscow: Progress.

Mayer-Schönberger, Viktor. 2009. *delete: The Virtue of Forgetting in the Digital Age*. Princeton: Princeton University Press.

McCloud, Scott. 1994. *Understanding Comics: The Invisible Art*. New York: Harper Perennial.

McCulloch, Warren S., and Walter Pitts. 1943. "A Logical Calculus of the Ideas Immanent in Nervous Activity." *Bulletin of Mathematical Biophysics* 5:115–33.

McGann, Jerome. 2001. *Radiant Textuality: Literature after the World Wide Web*. New York: Palgrave Macmillan.

McTaggart, J. Ellis. 1908. "The Unreality of Time." *Mind* 17, no. 68: 457–74.

Merchant, Carolyn. (1980) 1989. *The Death of Nature: Women, Ecology and the Scientific Revolution*. New York: HarperCollins.

Mitchell, Melanie. 2009. *Complexity: A Guided Tour*. Oxford: Oxford University Press.

Miyoshi, Masao, and Harry Harootunian, eds. 1989. *Postmodernism and Japan*. Durham: Duke University Press.

———, eds. 2002. *Learning Places: The Afterlives of Area Studies*. Durham: Duke University Press.

Mizuki Shigeru. 2013. *Showa: A History of Japan*. 4 vols. Translated by Zack Davisson. Montreal: Drawn and Quarterly.

Momigliano, Arnaldo. 1990. *The Classical Foundations of Modern Historiography*. Berkeley: University of California Press.

Mumford, Lewis. 1934. *Technics and Civilization*. New York: Harcourt, Brace.

———. 1964. "Authoritarian and Democratic Technics." *Technology and Culture* 5, no.1 (Winter): 1–8.

Munn, Nancy D. 1992. "The Cultural Anthropology of Time: A Critical Essay." *Annual Review of Anthropology* 21:91–123.

Musil, Robert. 1995. *The Man without Qualities*. Translated by Sophie Wilkins. New York: Alfred A. Knopf.

Najita, Tetsuo, and Irwin Scheiner, eds. 1978. *Japanese Thought in the Tokugawa Period, 1600–1868: Methods and Metaphors*. Chicago: University of Chicago Press.

Nead, Lynda. 2000. *Victorian Babylon: People, Streets and Images in Nineteenth-Century London*. New Haven: Yale University Press.

Negt, Oskar, and Alexander Kluge. 1993. *Public Sphere and Experience: Toward an Analysis of the Bourgeois and Proletarian Public Sphere*. Translated by Peter Labanyi, Jamie Owen Daniel, and Assenka Oksiloff. Minneapolis: University of Minnesota Press.

Newton, Isaac. (1687) 1995. *The Principia*. Translated by Andrew Motte. Amherst: Prometheus Books.

Nietzsche, Friedrich. 1983. "On the Uses and Disadvantages of History for Life." *Untimely Meditations*. Translated by R.J. Hollingdale, 57–123. Cambridge: Cambridge University Press.

Nisbet, Robert. 1980. *History of the Idea of Progress*. New York: Basic Books.

Norton, Robert E. 1991. *Herder's Aesthetics and the European Enlightenment*. Ithaca: Cornell University Press.

Novick, Peter. 1988. *That Noble Dream: The "Objectivity Question" and the American Historical Profession*. Cambridge: Cambridge University Press.

Nowotny, Helga. 1994. *Time: The Modern and Postmodern Experience*. Translated by Neville Plaice. Malden: Polity.

———. 2008. *Insatiable Curiosity: Innovation in a Fragile Future*. Translated by Mitch Cohen. Cambridge, MA: MIT Press.

———. 2016. *The Cunning of Uncertainty*. London: Polity.

Nunberg, Geoffrey. 1996. "Farewell to the Information Age." In *The Future of the Book*, edited by Geoffrey Nunberg, 103–38. Berkeley: University of California Press.

Nunez, Rafael, and Eve Sweetser. 2006. "With the Future behind Them: Convergent Evidence from Aymara Language and Gesture in the Crosslinguistic Comparison of Spatial Construals of Time." *Cognitive Science* 30:1–49.

O'Donnell, Daniel Paul. 2016. "A First Law of Humanities Computing." *Journal of Brief Ideas* (March 13), doi:10.5281/zenodo.47473.

Ogle, Vanessa. 2015. *The Global Transformation of Time: 1870–1950*. Cambridge, MA: Harvard University Press.

Okada, John. (1957) 1976. *No-No Boy*. Seattle: University of Washington Press.

Olsen, Niklas. 2012. *History in the Plural: An Introduction to the Work of Reinhart Koselleck*. New York: Berghahn Books.

Osborne, Peter. 1992. "Modernity Is a Qualitative, Not a Chronological, Category." *New Left Review* 1, no. 192: 65–84.

———. 2008. "Marx and the Philosophy of Time." *Radical Philosophy* 147:15–22.

Page, Scott. 2008. *The Difference: How the Power of Diversity Creates Better Groups, Firms, Schools, and Societies*. Princeton: Princeton University Press.

Parikka, Jussi. 2013. "Archival Media Theory: An Introduction to Wolfgang Ernst's Media Archaeology." In *Digital Memory and the Archive*, by Wolfgang Ernst. Edited by Jussi Parikka, 1–22. Minneapolis: University of Minnesota Press.

———. 2014. *The Anthrobscene*. Minneapolis: University of Minnesota Press.

Perovic, Sanja. 2017. "Dead History, Live Art: Encountering the Past with Stuart Brisley." *Rethinking History* 21, no. 2: 274–95.

Pias, Claus. 2016. "The Age of Cybernetics." In *Cybernetics: The Macy Conferences, 1946–1953*, edited by Claus Pias, 11–26. Zurich-Berlin: diaphanes.

Polanyi, Karl. (1944) 1957. *The Great Transformation*. Boston: Beacon Press.

Poovey, Mary. 1994. "Figures of Arithmetic, Figures of Speech: The Discourse of Statistics." In *Questions of Evidence: Proof, Practice, and Persuasion across Disciplines*, edited by James Chandler, Arnold I. Davidson, and Harry Harootunian, 401–21. Chicago: University of Chicago Press.

Postone, Moishe. 1993. *Time, Labor, and Social Domination: A Reinterpretation of Marx's Critical Theory*. Cambridge: Cambridge University Press.

Povinelli, Elizabeth A. 2002. *The Cunning of Recognition: Indigenous Alterities and the Making of Australian Multiculturalism*. Durham: Duke University Press.

Price, Derek J. de Solla. 1959. "On the Origin of Clockwork, Perpetual Motion Devices, and the Compass." *United States National Museum Bulletin 218: Contributions from the Museum of History and Technology*, Paper 6, 82–112. Washington, DC: Smithsonian Institution.

Prigogine, Ilya, and Isabelle Stengers. 1984. *Order out of Chaos: Man's New Dialogue with Nature*. London: Flamingo Paperbacks.

Rabinbach, Anson. 1990. *The Human Motor: Energy, Fatigue, and the Origins of Modernity*. New York: Basic Books.

Rancière, Jacques. 1994. *The Names of History: On the Poetics of Knowledge*. Translated by Hassan Melehy. Minneapolis: University of Minnesota Press.

Ranke, Leopold von. 1973. *The Theory and Practice of History*. Edited by Georg G. Iggers and Konrad von Moltke. Translated by Wilma A. Iggers and von Moltke. Indianapolis: Bobbs-Merrill.

Renan, Ernst. 1990. "What Is a Nation?" Translated and annotated by Martin Thom. In *Nation and Narration*, edited by Homi K. Bhabha, 8–22. London: Routledge.

Richards, E. G. 1998. *Mapping Time: The Calendar and Its History*. Oxford: Oxford University Press.

Rosa, Hartmut. 2003. "Social Acceleration: Ethical and Political Consequences of a Desynchronized High-Speed Society." *Constellations* 10, no. 1: 3–33.

Rosenblueth, Arturo, Norbert Wiener, and Julian Bigelow. 1943. "Behavior, Purpose and Teleology." *Philosophy of Science* 10, no. 1: 18–24.

Roth, Paul A. 2013. "The Silence of the Norms: The Missing Historiography of *The Structure of Scientific Revolutions*." *Studies in History and Philosophy of Science* 44:545–52.

Rovelli, Carlo. 2018. *The Order of Time*. Translated by Erica Segre and Simon Carnell. New York: Riverhead Books.

Runia, Eelco. 2014. *Moved by the Past: Discontinuity and Historical Mutation*. New York: Columbia University Press.

Rüsen, Jörn. 1995. "Social Change and the Development of Historiography—a Theoretical Approach." In *Understanding Social Change in the Nineties: Theoretical Approaches and Historiographical Perspectives*, edited by Valentin Váquez de Prada and Ignacio Olábarri, 111–26. Aldershot: Ashgate.

Rushkoff, Douglas. 2013. *Present Shock: When Everything Happens Now*. New York: Current.

Russell, Edmund. 2011. *Evolutionary History: Uniting History and Biology to Understand Life on Earth*. Cambridge: Cambridge University Press.

———. 2018. *Greyhound Nation: A Coevolutionary History of England, 1200–1900*. New York: Cambridge University Press.

Saussy, Haun. 2016. *The Ethnography of Rhythm: Orality and Its Technologies*. New York: Fordham University Press.

Schiffman, Zachary Sayre. 2011. *The Birth of the Past*. Baltimore: Johns Hopkins University Press.

Schivelbusch, Wolfgang. 1986. *The Railway Journey: Trains and Travel in the 19th Century*. Translated by Anselm Hollo. Berkeley: University of California Press.

Schrödinger, Erwin. (1944) 1967. *What Is Life*. Cambridge: Cambridge University Press.

Serres, Michel. 1995. "The Birth of Time." In *Genesis*, translated by Geneviève James and James Nielson, 81–122. Ann Arbor: University of Michigan Press.

Serres, Michel, with Bruno Latour. 1995. *Conversations on Science, Culture, and Time*. Translated by Roxanne Lapidus. Ann Arbor: University of Michigan Press.

Sewell, William H., Jr. 2008. "The Temporalities of Capitalism." *Socio-Economic Review* 6:517–37.

Shannon, Claude E., and Warren Weaver. 1949. *The Mathematical Theory of Communication*. Urbana: University of Illinois Press.

Shapin, Steven. 1996. *The Scientific Revolution*. Chicago: University of Chicago Press.

Sharma, Sarah. 2014. *In the Meantime: Temporality and Cultural Politics*. Durham: Duke University Press.

Sheehan, Jonathan, and Dror Wahrman. 2015. *Invisible Hands: Self-Organization and the Eighteenth Century*. Chicago: University of Chicago Press.

Shoemaker, Bob. 2015. "The Future of the (E)Book." *History Matters* (blog), December 1, 2015. http://www.historymatters.group.shef.ac.uk/future-ebook/.

Shyrock, Andrew, and Daniel Lord Smail. 2011. *Deep History: The Architecture of Past and Present*. Berkeley: University of California Press.

Simmel, Georg. (1900) 1990. *The Philosophy of Money*. Edited by David Frisby. Translated by Tom Bottomore and David Frisby. London: Routledge.

———. (1903) 2002. "The Metropolis and Mental Life." In *The Blackwell City Reader*, edited by Gary Bridge and Sophie Watson, 11–19. Malden, MA: Wiley-Blackwell.

Simon, Herbert A. 1962. "The Architecture of Complexity." *Proceedings of the American Philosophical Society* 106, no. 6 (December 12): 467–82.

Siskin, Clifford. 2016. *System: The Shaping of Modern Knowledge*. Cambridge, MA: MIT Press.

Smail, Daniel. 2008. *On Deep History and the Brain*. Berkeley: University of California Press.

Smith Rumsey, Abby. 2016. *When We Are No More: How Digital Memory Is Shaping Our Future*. New York: Bloomsbury Press.

Sousanis, Nick. 2015. *Unflattening*. Cambridge, MA: Harvard University Press.

Spiegel, Gabrielle M. 1997. *The Past as Text: The Theory and Practice of Medieval Historiography*. Baltimore: Johns Hopkins University Press.

Stafford, Barbara Maria. 2007. *Echo Objects: The Cognitive Work of Images*. Chicago: University of Chicago Press.

Stafford, Lorren, and Chris Strouth. 2001. "The Nature of Time." Track 1 on *Future Perfect: The Nature of Time*. Innova Recordings, compact disc.

Standage, Tom. 1999. *The Victorian Internet: The Remarkable Story of the Telegraph and the Nineteenth Century's On-Line Pioneers*. New York: Berkley Books.

———. 2013. *Writing on the Wall: Social Media—the First 2,000 Years*. New York: Bloomsbury.

Steffen, Will, Jacques Grinevald, Paul Crutzen, and John McNeill. 2011. "The Anthropocene: Conceptual and Historical Perspectives." *Philosophical Transactions of the Royal Society A* 369, no. 1938: 842–67.

Tanaka, Stefan. 1993. *Japan's Orient: Rendering Pasts into History*. Berkeley: University of California Press.

———. 2004. *New Times in Modern Japan*. Princeton: Princeton University Press.

Thomas, Keith. 1971. *Religion and the Decline of Magic: Studies in Popular Beliefs in Sixteenth and Seventeenth Century England*. London: Weidenfeld and Nicolson.

Thompson, E. P. 1967. "Time, Work-Discipline, and Industrial Capitalism." *Past and Present* 38, no. 1: 56–97.

Thrift, Nigel. 1999. "The Place of Complexity." *Theory, Culture & Society* 16, no. 3: 31–69.

Toews, John Edward. 2004. *Becoming Historical: Cultural Reformation and Public Memory in Early Nineteenth-Century Berlin*. Cambridge, UK: Cambridge University Press.

Tomba, Massimiliano. 2013. *Marx's Temporalities*. Translated by Peter D. Thomas and Sara R. Farris. Chicago: Haymarket Books.

Toulmin, Stephen, and June Goodfield. 1965. *The Discovery of Time*. Chicago: University of Chicago Press.

Traub, Valerie. 2013. "The New Unhistoricism in Queer Studies." *PMLA* 128, no. 1: 21–39.

Turkle, Sherry. 2011. *Alone Together: Why We Expect More from Technology and Less from Each Other*. New York: Basic Books.

Twenge, Jean M. 2017. *iGen: Why Today's Super-Connected Kids Are Growing Up Less Rebellious, More Tolerant, Less Happy—and Completely Unprepared for Adulthood*. New York: Atria Books.

van Dijck, José. 2014. "Datafication, Dataism and Dataveillance: Big Data between Scientific Paradigm and Ideology." *Surveillance & Society* 12, no. 2: 197–208.

Varela, Francisco. 1992. "Making It Concrete: Before, during and after Breakdowns." In *Revisioning Philosophy*, edited by James Ogilvy, 97–109. Albany: State University of New York Press.

Vester, Frederic. 1979. "Time and Biology." In *Time and the Sciences*, edited by J. M. Abraham and Frank Greenaway, 53–70. Paris: UNESCO.

Vismann, Cornelia. 2008. *Files: Law and Media Technology*. Translated by Geoffrey Winthrop-Young. Stanford: Stanford University Press.

von Foerster, Heinz. (1979) 2003. "Cybernetics of Cybernetics." In *Understanding Understanding: Essays on Cybernetics and Cognition*, edited by von Foerster, 283–86. New York: Springer-Verlag.

———. 2014. *The Beginning of Heaven and Earth Has No Name: Seven Days with Second-Order Cybernetics*. Edited by Albert Müller and Karl H. Müller. Translated by Elinor Rooks and Michael Kasenbacher. New York: Fordham University Press.

Vygotsky, L. S. 1978. *Mind in Society: The Development of Higher Psychological Processes*. Edited by Michael Cole, Vera John-Steiner, Sylvia Scribner, and Ellen Souberman. Cambridge, MA: Harvard University Press.

Wagner, Peter. 2016. *Progress: A Reconstruction*. Cambridge: Polity.

Weaver, Warren. 1948. "Science and Complexity." *American Scientist* 36, no. 4: 536–44.

Wertsch, James V., ed. 1985a. *Culture, Communication, and Cognition: Vygotskian Perspectives*. Cambridge: Cambridge University Press.

——. 1985b. *Vygotsky and the Social Formation of Mind*. Cambridge, MA: Harvard University Press.

Wineberg, Sam. 2001. *Historical Thinking and Other Unnatural Acts*. Philadelphia: Temple University Press.

White, Hayden. 1973. *Metahistory: The Historical Imagination in Nineteenth-Century Europe*. Baltimore: Johns Hopkins University Press.

——. 1978. "The Fictions of Factual Representation." In *Tropics of Discourse: Essays in Cultural Criticism*, 121–34. Baltimore: Johns Hopkins University Press.

——. 1987. "The Value of Narrativity in Representation of Reality." In *The Content of the Form: Narrative Discourse and Historical Representation*, 1–25. Baltimore: Johns Hopkins University Press.

——. 2014. *The Practical Past*. Evanston: Northwestern University Press.

White, Richard. 1998. *Remembering Ahanagran: Storytelling in a Family's Past*. New York: Hill and Wang.

Whitehead, Alfred North. 1925. *Science and the Modern World*. New York: Free Press.

Wiener, Norbert. 1950. *Human Use of Human Beings: Cybernetics and Society*. Boston: Houghton Mifflin.

Winchester, Simon. 2001. *The Map That Changed the World*. New York: HarperCollins.

Wilcox, Donald J. 1987. *The Measure of Times Past*. Chicago: University of Chicago Press.

Wishnitzer, Avner. 2015. *Reading Clocks, Alla Turca: Time and Society in the Late Ottoman Empire*. Chicago: University of Chicago Press.

Wolf, Maryanne. 2008. *Proust and the Squid: The Story and Science of the Reading Brain*. New York: Harper Perennial.

Wolin, Sheldon. 1997. "What Time Is It?" *Theory & Event* 1, no. 1. https://muse.jhu.edu/.

Yerushalmi, Yosef Hayim. (1982) 1996. *Zakhor: Jewish History and Jewish Memory*. Seattle: University of Washington Press.

Young, Marilyn B. 2012. "'I Was Thinking, as I Often Do These Days, of War': The United States in the Twenty-First Century." *Diplomatic History* 36, no. 1 (January): 1–15.

Young, Michael. 1988. *The Metronomic Society: Natural Rhythms and Human Timetables*. Cambridge, MA: Harvard University Press.

Zalasiewicz, Jan, Mark Williams, Alan Haywood, and Michael Ellis. 2011. "The Anthropocene: A New Epoch of Geological Time?" *Philosophical Transactions of the Royal Society* 369:835–41.

Zammito, John. 2009. "Herder and Historical Metanarrative: What's Philosophical about History?" In *A Companion to the Works of Johann Gottfried Herder*, edited by Hans Adler and Wulf Koepke, 65–91. Martlesham: Boydell and Brewer.

Zammito, John H., Karl Menges, and Ernest A. Menze. 2010. "Johann Gottfried Herder Revisited: The Revolution in Scholarship in the Last Quarter Century." *Journal of the History of Ideas* 71, no. 4: 661–84.

Zielinski, Siegfried. 2006. *Deep Time of the Media: Toward an Archaeology of Hearing and Seeing by Technical Means*. Translated by Gloria Custance. Cambridge, MA: MIT Press.

Notes

INTRODUCTION

1. Chronology, as I use it, refers to the passage along a linear and regular timeline based on the idea of absolute time. It is the time reckoning system that we use throughout much of the globe today. For a critique and modification, see Jordheim (forthcoming) for his equally provocatively titled essay, "Return to Chronology."

2. Schrödinger offers a brief and thoughtful description of the limitation of using physical laws to describe biological processes ([1944] 1967: 76–85).

3. Long ago, Hayden White pointed to the rich work of historians throughout the nineteenth century, which in the end remained within a discursive whole. He writes that the various tropes "have permitted me to view the various debates over how history ought to be written, which occurred throughout the nineteenth century, as essentially matters of stylistic variation within a single universe of discourse" (1973: 427).

4. I have relied on the Lukács translation. The account in the *Collected Works* translates this phrase as "time's carcase" (Marx 1976: 127). The use of *carcase* is common and goes back at least to H. Quelch's translation (Marx 1900: 25) where he uses "carcase of time." I read *incarnation* (or *embodiment*) to be closer to the German: "Die Zeit is alles, der Mensch is nichts mehr, er is höchstens noch die Verkörperung der Zeit" (Marx 1974: 85).

5. Digital humanities has been especially strong in building tools and approaches that facilitate and enhance analog modes of analysis. For a fine critique that suggests (like this book) that digital humanists must go further into conceptual and other realms, see Kleinberg (2017), especially chapter 4.

6. The implementation of this transition provides an example of my discussion on change in chapter 4. Change is not linear or a replacement but involves legacy structures, entrenched cultural practices, multiple rhythms, and attempted disruption. For a description of a similar but bolder case, see Shoemaker 2015.

7. I realize that the word *information* has more ambiguity than *fact* or *data*. I use it though for that reason. It has portability, an aura of autonomy, and (almost contradictorily) the suggestion of social situatedness. Above all, it is important to recognize these variations as we use it. Geoffrey Nunberg (1996) has a fine analysis of the word.

8. The compression of time-space has been occurring since the mid-nineteenth century, beginning with the railroad (Schivelbusch 1986) and the telegraph (Standage 1999; Kittler 1990).

9. In his essay "A Mathematical Theory of Communication," first published in *The Bell System Technical Journal* in 1948, Shannon wrote, "The fundamental problem of communication is that of reproducing at one point either exactly or approximately a message selected at another point. Frequently the messages have *meaning*. . . . These semantic aspects of communication are irrelevant to the engineering problem" (Shannon and Weaver 1949: 3). This technical essay was republished with Weaver's explanation in the book *The Mathematical Theory of Communication*. Weaver brings the level down a notch from that of the mathematician to describe the relation between this technical problem in relation to semantics and effectiveness (95–117). Wolfgang Ernst described a similar process of separation in his work on the archive where artifacts were "desemioticized" and then subjected to a "process of resemiosis" to support the narrative of the nation (2002: 108).

10. I recognize that throughout the twentieth century, there were many quite important efforts to bridge these knowledge systems. Overall, though, they have been marginalized if not forgotten.

11. I first became aware of Kuhn's statement in Fasolt's important and provocative book (2004).

12. Paul Roth frames Kuhn's statement, pointing out that while Kuhn describes history as an explanatory enterprise, its narrative form or structure is hidden (2013: 550).

13. For a fine critique that recognizes both Benjamin's quest for an alternative to this time and Ben Anderson's misreading of this phrase as "being," not "critique," see Davis (2010: 60–63). Lorenz (2017: 118–19) argues that "empty" time did not exist during the European Middle Ages.

14. For a fine essay on *historia magistra vitae*, see Koselleck (1985: 21–38).

15. Historians have been questioning progress and considering multiple forms of change for decades. See, for example, Cole and Smith 2010; Shapin 1996; and Wagner 2016.

16. For example, writings that conceive of the past as a foreign country would not be conceivable prior to this application of absolute time. See, for example, Lowenthal (1985).

17. In his appeal to reappraise mystics, Certeau writes, "A set of new social and theoretical interests transforms the way *mystics* appears in the field of our interrogation. To specify that relation is to exhume the present postulates of our analyses and explore the issue of what work that past experience performs in our epistemological sites. It is to 'historicize' our research in placing it back into a contemporary configuration on which it is dependent, and to 'dehistoricize' *mystics* in showing that one cannot reduce it to a past positivity. In exploring what our sciences *do* with *mystics*, we also recognize what it *writes into* them" (2015: 9).

18. For a wonderful history that helped me think about this issue, see Edgerton (2007), where he discusses technological development through utility (e.g., donkeys and horses in World War I and corrugated metal throughout the twentieth century).

19. At the outset of *The Writing of History*, Certeau quotes Alphonse Dupront: "'The sole historical quest for "meaning" remains indeed a quest for the Other,' but, however contradictory it may be, this project aims at 'understanding' and, through 'meaning,' at hiding the alterity of this foreigner; or, in what amounts to the same thing, it aims at calming the dead who still haunt the present, and at offering them scriptural tombs" (1988: 2). For a statement on the relation of chronological time to classification, see his epigraph in chapter 2.

20. His actual words are the following: "It is only in appearance that the 'facts' in such a case speak for themselves, alone, exclusively, 'objectively.' Without the narrator to make them speak, they would be dumb" (Droysen 1967: 52–53).

CHAPTER ONE: TIME HAS A HISTORY

1. For a wonderful critique of linear historical thinking, see Ermarth (2011).

2. The writings are now vast. There are many important works today; I will not recount them here. Some of the most important influences on my thinking are Adam, Nowotny, Fraser, Wilcox, Certeau, Koselleck, Luckmann, Hartog, Runia, and Spiegel.

3. I am indebted to Geof Bowker for bringing this essay to my attention.

4. I have relied on the work of Mali and Blumenberg for my understanding of myth. Mali calls myth the "practical verities in which the members of the community all believe and live" (2003: 4).

5. There are many good works on this history. Beyond what I have already mentioned, David Landes's *Revolution in Time* is a classic, especially in connection to clocks. The books of Barbara Adam have helped broaden and steady my understanding. Toulmin and Goodfield's *The Discovery of Time* for quite a while seemed to be a standard, and I still return to Donald Wilcox's *The Measure of Times Past*.

6. This would be a long list. A good start for history is the reference-like work of Richards, and I have frequently returned to Wilcox. In anthropology, Munn has a fine overview, and Birth has a more recent account. Fabian remains one of the best conceptual critiques, and Povinelli has brought a much more layered and conceptual understanding of multiple times and otherness.

7. In his work on Bali, Clifford Geertz succinctly described the significance of the calendar: "They don't tell you what time it is; they tell you what kind of time it is" (1973: 393).

8. According to F. C. Haber, the purpose of early clocks was less to tell the time than to represent the motions of the heavens; it was a machine harmonized with religion (1975: 399). Price argues that the early mechanical clocks should be seen within a lineage of astronomical devices that go back to the Antikythera mechanism, not the sundial and clepsydra (1959).

9. Throughout this book, I will use the abbreviations for "before Christ" and "anno Domini." Using these names, in my mind, is more accurate to the history of time; our linear time was connected to the church, and declaring it as common only seeks to naturalize the particularity of this reckoning of time, hiding its historicity.

10. Dionysus was four years off. Most scholars now date the birth of Christ in 4 BC.

11. For a more detailed account, see Wilcox (1987: 187–220).

12. Previous to the Meiji *ishin* one reign often had several *nengo*. Following the *ishin*, the reign and *nengo* became the same, an "invented tradition."

13. I will discuss below the way that such conclusions—as an earlier moment of the modern—themselves are conditioned by modern chronology.

14. Barbara Adam (2004: 76) writes, "While there is no doubt that the temporal relations of archaic societies are different from those of 'modern' societies, we will see that they are no less complex, sophisticated or temporally extended." In the next chapter, I will discuss how this separation of old from modern is essential to the maintenance of the modern.

15. Michael Young writes, "Habit is not only the most precious conservative agent of society, it is also its opposite, its most precious radical agent, enabling us to pay attention to new departures" (1988: 124).

16. This statement is taken from Newton's definition of time in the Scholium of *The Principia* ([1687] 1995: 13).

17. We have come a long way: A fourteenth-century church document responds to the validity of what we now call interest: "In doing so he would be selling time and would be committing usury by selling what does not belong to him" (Le Goff 1980: 29). Le Goff is clear that we must be careful to see this not as proof of a secular/religious divide but as a transition to multiple understandings of time and changing society.

18. For example, Nicholas Malebranche used another new technology, mathematics, to measure relations between units (Schiffman 2011: 228–33).

19. I will discuss this notion of duration below. Newton's duration is an activity between two points; this is a measurement that spatializes time. See also Adam (1990: 54–55).

20. This emphasis on the clock keeps our understanding of time within Newtonian physics. When we bring in other times—for example, that of energy use and of biological organisms—it becomes possible to move beyond physical time. This will be discussed later in this chapter and in chapter 4.

21. For an interesting criticism of how clock time imbricates intellectual life, see Levy (2007). The Slow Movement is an interesting effort that emerged in the 1980s to counter the ways that this accelerating time dominates the way we live. It started as a protest against the building of a McDonald's fast-food restaurant near the Piazza di Spagna in Rome. A bowl of penne became the symbol of this movement.

22. See, for example, Glennie and Thrift (2009); Nead (2000).

23. The various ages of man describe the growth of man in relation to stages connected to world view. These stages recognize the life course but are not developmental.

24. Locke did not believe all men were capable, only gentlemen. Moreover, women had different roles (and abilities) in his scheme.

25. Darwin's (1877) observations of his son are a fascinating read. For us, his descriptions are obvious, even naive, but his essay was important in fostering an understanding of child development in the latter half of the nineteenth century.

26. The use of mathematics in this discovery of the past and future were the components of what Alfred North Whitehead called the historical revolt, the use of history to revolt against the authority of the divine. He wrote

that the historical revolt "is the divination of some characteristics of a particular future from the known characteristics of a particular past" (1925: 44).

27. Bowker points out that Lyell's geology was not structured linearly but was built on cyclical action (Bowker 2005: 53–62). See also Winchester (2001).

28. For recent work that discusses the synchronization of non-Western places to this world time, see Barak (2013), Ogle (2015), Tanaka (2004) and Wishnitzer (2015).

29. Serres writes, "When a system expands, in dimension, number, and complexity, it always has a tendency to form into subsets" (1995: 84).

30. A terrific example of Lefebvre's moments is in Meiji Japan and the Japanese historiography that celebrates the desire for and success of Japan's transition into a modern state, illustrated with the slogan "Fukoku, kyōhei" (Rich country, strong military).

31. Even though space has gained an elevated status in academia as a discrete mode of analysis, my reading of geographers such as Entriken, Harvey, Lefebvre, and Sack brought me to understand that space in modern society is the stoppage or slowing of time (see, for example, Lefebvre 1991: 84–85, 94–96). In his introduction to *Rhythmanalysis*, Stuart Elden argues that the reading of Lefebvre as spatial overlooks the historical and temporal dimensions of his writings (Lefebvre 2004: ix.)

32. Many scholars—for example, Certeau, Chakrabarty, Fabian, Harootunian, Marx, and Sharma—have pointed out that the primitive is the other that reinforces the view that the modern is always advanced.

33. Whitehead states, "Classification is the halfway house between the immediate concreteness of the individual thing and the complete abstraction of mathematical notions" (1925: 28).

34. Bergson writes, "In order that the number should go on increasing in proportion as we advance, we must retain the successive images and set them alongside each of the new units which we picture to ourselves: now, it is in space that such a juxtaposition takes place and not in pure duration. In fact, it will be easily granted that counting material objects means thinking all these objects together, thereby leaving them in space" ([1913] 2001: 77).

35. Georg Lukács writes that time "freezes into an exactly delimited, quantifiable continuum filled with quantifiable things . . . in short, it becomes space" (quoted in Gross 1982: 64). I will be discussing a different notion of duration in chapter 3.

36. One can, of course, dispute Whitehead's argument, yet to do so goes against recent (twentieth-century) science—in particular, relativity and quantum mechanics and some social sciences, especially those of cognition.

37. Later, he writes, "We shall see that time, conceived under the form of an unbounded and homogeneous medium, is nothing but the ghost of space haunting the reflective consciousness" (Bergson [1913] 2001: 99). This is akin to Certeau's discussion of tombs.

38. The transcription of the second five meetings of the Macy Conferences is a wonderful read on the effort of scientists to integrate cognition into a mechanical (physics) understanding of the brain (Pias 2016).

39. One of the problems of this formulation is that periods and nation-states become the naturalized containers, the "mass" that then must be filled in by history. The "becoming" is only a becoming of something that has a naturalized status.

40. Siskin uses a form of text mining where he looks at the title pages of *Eighteenth Century Collections Online* to discern the propensity of words appearing in the same title as the word *system*. He finds that between 1700 and 1739, *history* and *system* are distant, with *ancient* and *modern* more likely to appear with *system*. Between 1740 and 1779, he finds greater likelihood, but in the final two decades of the century (1779–1800), *system*, *history*, *ancient*, and *modern* are adjacent to each other (2016: 49–52).

41. If we measure the founding of a discipline through the formation of its national society, we see that the disciplines emerge as absolute time is superseded. The Modern Language Association was founded in 1883, the American Historical Association in 1884, the American Anthropological Association in 1902, the American Political Science Association in 1903, and the American Sociological Association in 1905.

42. For a description of proper time, see J. T. Fraser's forward to Nowotny's *Time*, whose German title is *Eigenzeit*.

43. Until recently, one of the few social scientists to apply entropy is Georgescu-Roegen (1986), an economist. I am indebted to Keith Pezzoli for bringing this intellectual to my attention. The work of Jennifer Gabrys (2011) invokes a Benjaminian-style natural history (as opposed to Darwin and evolution) that examines waste and decay. The media archaeologist Wolfgang Ernst (2002) uses entropy to build his interpretation of the archives, especially in relation to digital media.

44. Three papers stimulated the conference. They were McCulloch and Pitts (1943); Rosenblueth, Wiener, and Bigelow (1943); and Shannon and Weaver

(1949). There are several fine accounts of these conferences (Heims 1980, 1991; Dupuy 2000; and Hayles 1999).

45. The title was changed following the sixth conference in 1949. *Cybernetics* is the title of one of Norbert Wiener's books; etymologically it is from the Greek, translated as "steersman."

46. In many ways, it was the foundational moment for today's emphasis on the STEM fields.

47. For a map showing genealogies of complex systems, see Brian Castellani (2013). I began this inquiry into complex systems through researchers connected to the Santa Fe Institute. I decided to focus on cybernetics and general system theory to draw attention to the potential for not just complex relations—usually applied to the social sciences as networks—but also how they bring a different epistemology and multiple times into our conceptual structure and understandings of society. For a recent effort to bring these ideas to the humanities and human sciences, see Clarke and Hansen (2009).

CHAPTER TWO: HISTORY HAS A HISTORY

1. Big History extends the past to the Big Bang. The Anthropocene is a proposed epoch that incorporates human impact on earth systems.

2. I hope that the Anthropocene will not be subsumed and can remain a separate but converging layer, but Chakrabarty's recent discussion on Anthropocene time shows the difficulty of moving beyond what he calls world history (2018).

3. I could actually begin my narrative with Herodotus. In contrast to the narratives that locate Herodotus as the father of history as a descriptive media, recent research has emphasized the multivocality, multiplicity, and relationality in his work, as well as his emphasis on communication. Egbert J. Bakker writes, "'History' for him is not an object of study, something you write, or write about; it is an intellectual tool and a communication activity" (2002: 3).

4. The *Kojiki* is the earliest extant text (completed in 712) of the mythical and historical rule of emperors and empresses in what we now call Japan. Rather than a "history," it is closer to a genealogy described below.

5. Collingwood (1994: 257–61) derisively calls such histories "scissors-and-paste" history.

6. For a recent argument on the value of such a singular time, see Le Goff (2015: 9). Importantly, Le Goff understands many of the problems wrought by a unified time but argues that the benefits are greater.

7. Having just read recent predictions on sea-level rise, Newton might be more accurate than I care to believe.

8. The analogy of physical mass and units of people becomes possible with the rise of aggregation described in the previous chapter.

9. For example, Montesquieu stated, "For the occasions which produce great changes are different, but, since men had the same passions at all times, the causes are always the same" (quoted in Schiffman 2011: 258). According to Schiffman, his past was essential for "the importance of context for understanding all things human" (263).

10. I will return to this in chapter 4. In her thoughtful extended essay *The Cunning of Uncertainty* (2016), Helga Nowotny's call for a global contextualism echoes some of the characteristics of Herder's cosmopolitanism. This is an example of thinking about modernity as the anomaly, where the thinking prior to modernity has similarity to the situated and heterogeneous thinking of today. To paraphrase Zielinski's words, this is where we might find the new in the old (2006).

11. As Toulmin and Goodfield point out, this grounding of heterogeneity and historical change in race is, of course, wrought with potential for racist theories. German national socialists emphasized the racial dimension to justify their ideas, but Toulmin and Goodfield show that his writing is cosmopolitanism (Toulmin and Goodfield 1965: 139). It is fascinating that though Herder created greater space for heterogeneity, his world system was still ordered with Asia at the earlier level, Greece and Rome next, and then with Germany. For a recent reappraisal of Herder, see Zammito, Menges, and Menze (2010).

12. Peter Osborne (1992) argues that modernity is a qualitative, not chronological category.

13. I interpret these statements as truisms that have little use except to obfuscate notions of repetition and change. Change will be discussed in chapter 4.

14. In the social sciences, it is known as development; in biology, it is evolution. In technology, it was progress and is now innovation. Here, this mechanical, linear time becomes natural, an externality that exists.

15. For an example of a work that critiques the structure yet ultimately reinforces it, see my *Japan's Orient* (Tanaka 1993).

16. Echoing Hegel's world history, Ranke exclaims in the essay "On the Character of Historical Science" that "India had philosophy; she did not have history," as if that were factual (Ranke 1973: 34).

17. Kathleen Davis (2010: 52) points to the similarity of the way that history positions the Middle Ages and Europe's non-Western others. Both are prior and different.

18. Serres writes, "History is thus the projection of this very real exclusion into an imaginary, even imperialistic time. The temporal rupture is the equivalent

of a dogmatic expulsion" (Serres with Latour 1995: 50). For Marx and formal subsumption, see Tomba (2013) and Harootunian (2015).

19. Povinelli's discussion is on recognition and experience rather than linear history. It is a rich discussion, especially in thinking beyond either the dominant or the victim, where recognition invokes experience as well as conditions of espionage and camouflage (2002: 76–79).

20. Certeau writes, "The 'same' is a historical *form*, a practice of dichotomy, and not a homogeneous *content*" (1992: 18).

21. For example, Fukuzawa Yukichi, the intellectual celebrated for his enlightened (i.e., Western-oriented) views, lamented the previous state of society in his famous *An Outline of a Theory of Civilization*, "Therefore, throughout the whole twenty-five centuries or so of Japanese history, the government has been continually doing the same thing; it is like reading the same book over and over again, or presenting the same play time after time" ([1874] 1973: 142). Japan, with more than a millennium of recorded pasts, had no history.

22. In a very different field, the media theorist Marsha Kinder remarked that she was reluctant to date her ethnographic notes because of the way that dating signifies "objective detachment" (1991: 24–25).

23. For a concise critique of this emphasis on facts as objective, see White (1978).

24. She writes, "The aim was to 'cleanse' the facts to be able to put them on a solid foundation of proof that is stripped of their original context and thus generally valid" (2008: 16).

25. In Japan, the discipline of national literature emerged simultaneously with the historical discipline. For a description of a similar process transforming medieval texts, see Wilcox (1987: 137–42).

26. See, for example, his "Preface Universal History" (Ranke 1973: 160–64). For Ranke, the way to this universal history was through the specificity of national histories. Ranke died before he completed this manuscript.

27. When the British Association for the Advancement of Science was founded in 1831, statistics was not accepted, primarily claiming that it lacked theoretical basis and was influenced by values of its practitioners (Poovey 1994: 401)

28. For a fine discussion of the way that archives support the rule of the liberal state, see Joyce (1999).

29. Work that pays attention to recent findings in cognitive fields is a growing and important area. For a good beginning, see Wolf (2008) for work on reading, Vygotsky (1978) for interaction and learning, and Hutchins (1995) for distributed cognition. For examples of works that explore the ways that these fields alter the humanities (and vice versa), see Stafford (2007) for cognition

and visuality, Connolly (2002) for connection to politics, and Smail (2008) for rethinking subjects of history.

INTERLUDE

1. It is interesting to consider the similarity between history and its purpose and Norbert Wiener's definition of cybernetics as "the study of messages as a means of controlling machines and society" (1950: 15).
2. An important exception to this conclusion is Caroline Arni, who on several occasions attempted to raise questions about history itself, categories of analysis, and the politics of time.
3. I am indebted to Sally Deutsch for bringing this work to my attention.

CHAPTER THREE: HETEROGENEOUS PASTS

1. For a discussion of unevenness, see Jameson (2003: 699–701).
2. Some scholars today are turning to "natural history" or "deep time" to avoid the limitations of chronology. See, for example, Gabrys (2011), Parikka (2014), and Russell (2011). We can also extend this search to the cognitive sciences. Humberto Maturana writes, "Living systems are cognitive systems, and living, as a process, is a process of cognition" (quoted in Clarke 2014: ix).
3. Herder's emphasis on national language and race has been cited as a "romantic" aberration. Moreover, his rejuvenation by Nazi's to support their argument for purity certainly taints him.
4. Rainer Wisbert comments on Herder, "Man is a unity of feelings, imagination and understanding and in all his powers—and this is the decisive—a creature of historicity" (quoted in Zammito, Menges, and Menze 2010: 665).
5. Herder writes, "Nature's year is long; the blooms of her plants are as many as these growths themselves and as the elements that nourish them. In India, Egypt, China, that has come to pass which nowhere and never will again come to pass on the earth; and so in Canaan, Greece, Rome, Carthage. The law of necessity and congruity, which is composed of potencies and place and time, everywhere brings forth different fruits" (quoted in Toulmin and Goodfield 1965: 139).
6. David Allen's very influential *Getting Things Done* is an example of this mechanization, or the Taylorization, of the mind.
7. Fraser indicates the limits of the analogy of recent physics to social forms. He argues that "time in the physical world is so primitive that it cannot accommodate the idea of a present with respect to which one could speak of a

future and a past" (1987: 222). For a more optimistic view from a quantum physicist, see Rovelli (2018).

8. There are numerous important works in this area. See, for example, Daniel Kahneman's *Thinking, Fast and Slow* (2011), McTaggart's classic essay (1908), and Alfred Gell's *The Anthropology of Time* (1992).

9. Alterity and otherness tend to be conflated; they are related. I follow the work of Levinas (1969), Blumenberg (1985), and Buber (1970), who distinguish between a dualistic self and other and a process of interaction where the self (and other) are in constant flux, the face to face.

10. I have chosen to continue this system. BC and AD, after all, fit my argument better than the current use of BCE and CE, an effort to naturalize the Christian chronology.

11. Confusion did exist, showing the problems of synchronization. The 1896 Olympics in Athens was held March 25–April 3 (Julian) or April 6–15 (Gregorian). The US team planned to arrive two weeks early for preparation, but when it arrived in Italy, it learned that Greece was still on the Julian, rushed to Greece, and barely made the event. The 1908 Russian team was twelve days late for the London Olympics in 1908. To bring this closer to today, the Mars Climate Orbiter crashed into the Martian atmosphere (1999) because system engineers used two standards: US (foot pounds) and metric (newton).

12. Schiffman argues that a key moment was in the writings of Montesquieu. He writes, "The commitment to understanding any given entity from *within* its context derived from an analytical view of the world that contextualized from *without*, by gauging the differences between entities" (2011: 209).

13. Fasolt writes, "Only the faith that some real boundary exists between the present and the past lends plausibility to the belief that historians can actually place things past into the context of 'their' time and place" (2004: 12).

14. For a description of the hierarchy in complex systems, see Simon (1962: 468–69) or Mitchell (2009).

15. See, for example, Guldi and Armitage (2014), who sought to address recent attacks against humanistic study and a decline of history enrollments, arguing that historians should embrace new methods, especially digital technologies and Big Data, to explore pasts beyond traditional time frames. A rather vitriolic critique by Deborah Cohen and Peter Mandler (2015) followed. For my purpose, the debate is over the boundary markers (beginning and end) and the nature of the content, spatialized time.

16. In 1958, Braudel reflected on the impact of the *longue durée*: "In all logic, this orchestration of conjunctures (political and social), by transcending itself,

should have led us straight to the *longue durée*. But for a thousand reasons this transcendence has not been the rule, and a return to the short term is being accomplished even now before our very eyes" (1980: 30).

17. See, for example, a wonderful video produced by Claire L. Evans, "The Evolution of the Earth in Sixty Seconds" (Lores 2009), which literally punctuates the shortness of the history of humans, let alone the Anthropocene.

18. For an inquiry that takes up the Anthropocene but operates using different times, see Parikka (2014). I find the work that invokes "deep time" to be more willing to question the ordering and classing propensities of classical time. See, for example, Smail (2008), Zielinski (2006), and Parikka (2013).

19. Young writes, "Initially, I wrote about all these [wars] as if war and peace were discrete: prewar, war, peace, or postwar. Over time, this progression of wars has looked to me less like a progression than a continuation: as if between one war and the next, the country was on hold" (2012: 1).

20. In psychology, an important thread is the work that translates the ideas of Lev Vygotsky for US psychological sciences. See Cole (1985), Wertsch (1985a, 1985b), and Vygotsky (1978).

21. See especially the work of Edwin Hutchins.

22. I am thankful to Harry Harootunian for bringing this classic to my attention.

23. In my reading, they develop this idea independently of Lave and Wenger (1991), which in my mind further supports the similarity across disciplines, especially the shift away from categories of being to activities that constitute groupings or categories.

24. This is a particularly apt term coined by Jonathan Walton in my seminar, the Politics of Time.

25. McGann writes, "The simplicity of the computer is merciless. It will expose every jot and tittle of your thought's imprecisions" (2001: 142).

26. History has generally ignored this understanding of time. See, for example, Novick 1988: 134–43; Liakos (2017: 144–45).

27. For a discussion of how the document narrows the archive of history, see Smail (2008: 43–66).

28. The one paper that directly addresses the observer is Laurence S. Kubie's paper "The Neurotic Potential and Human Adaptation" (Pias 2016: 66–97). For a fine description of the problem of the observer in cybernetics, see Hayles (1999: 73–80).

29. Bertalanffy explained psycho-physical organization: "Thus what is seen depends on our apperception, on our line of attention and interest which, in turn, is determined by training" (1968: 236).

30. I recognize the debate that has surfaced in reaction to Marcus. A key issue in that debate, perhaps the central one, is whether deep learning should work with the cognitive sciences.

31. Certeau, though, in criticism describes this well: "Historiography tends to prove that the site of its production can encompass the past: it is an odd procedure that posits death, a breakage everywhere reiterated in discourse, and that yet denies loss by appropriating to the present the privilege of recapitulating the past as a form of knowledge" (1988: 5).

32. What shall we call these? They are accounts, often rather narrative, of historic matter. See, for example, Doxiadis and Papadimitriou (2009). They include pictures; thus are they historical comics?

33. See, for example, Scott McCloud's discussion of the multiple temporalities, pacing, and motion possible in comics (1994: 94–117). In *Unflattening*, Nick Sousanis (2015) uses the comic to argue that textual narratives are "flat" and that greater nuance and more dimensions are possible in the comic medium.

34. This is especially evident in Foley's website, http://pathwaysproject.org. The electronic site uses the affordances of the technology to show relations. The same networked topics in the book are organized alphabetically. The juxtaposition between print text and electronic print demonstrates the affordances of electronic media where, in the words of Bolter and Grusin (2000: 34), "the logic of hypermediacy multiplies the signs of mediation and in this way tries to reproduce the rich sensorium of human experience." It is debatable whether Foley succeeds, but the contrast to print demonstrates well its limitations.

35. For a sophisticated and honest appraisal of the false certainties in our current system and a wonderful meditation on the possibilities that can emerge from this weakening of previous certitudes, see Nowotny (2016).

36. Certeau finds this characteristic in de Cusa, who "devoted himself to *thinking potentiality* in terms of *positions* defined by a *reciprocal determination*" (2015: 28).

CHAPTER FOUR: CHANGE AND HISTORY

1. DeLanda calls this form of reification "taxonomic essentialisms" (2006: 28).

2. Bergson describes this cognitive process, the spatialization of time: "We need immobility, and the more we succeed in imagining movement as coinciding with the immobilities of the points of space through which it passes, the better we think we understand it" (2002: 257).

3. I think of Augé's description of the airport as "supermodernity's" nonplace, a nowhere we pass through, in solitude. Sharma (2014) reminds us that circulation is only possible through the production of and dependence on marginalized temporalities, especially that of labor.

4. I use the twentieth century because the understanding of time that follows is from the late nineteenth and twentieth centuries. This is still much more recent than seventeenth-century Newtonian time.

5. For a fine analysis that brings entropy to considerations of time in social theory, see Adam (1990, especially chapter 2).

6. For a trenchant analysis of ways that economics ignores thermodynamics, see Georgescu-Roegen (1986). Recently, scholars in the humanities (Ernst, Parikka) and social sciences (Gabrys) have incorporated entropy in their analyses.

7. The original title was (and it still makes me pause) "Feedback Mechanisms and Circular Causal Systems in Biological and Social Systems."

8. Bertalanffy writes, "It can be shown that the *primary* regulations in organic systems . . . are of the nature of dynamic interaction. They are based upon the fact that the living organism is an open system, maintaining itself in, or approaching a steady state. Superposed are those regulations which we may call *secondary*, and which are controlled by fixed arrangements, especially of the feedback type" (1968: 44).

9. For a good description of homeostasis, see Michael Young (1988: 37–40).

10. Smail juxtaposed the Darwinian biological model to the Lamarkian model of cultural influence (ontogeny vs. philogeny) to question intention and causality. Instead, he argued for "blind variation and selective retention" (2008: 111).

11. In his new book, Russell (2018) shows the coevolutionary process through a study of greyhounds in England.

12. DeLanda writes, "The identity of any assemblage at any level of scale is always the product of a process . . . and it is always precarious, since other processes can destabilize it" (2006: 28).

13. We are the only major industry in the twenty-first century of which I am familiar that gives away intellectual property to businesses and corporations that then charge us for access to what we gave away! It is actually worse than this sounds.

14. For a provocative work that thinks of the Anthropocene through entropy, see Parikka (2014).

15. Chakrabarty (2018) points to a fundamental difficulty in Anthropocene time, the copresence and tension between a world history and an earth history. An

epistemological shift is necessary to move from the human-centered to an earth-centered form of knowledge and problem solving.

16. Jordheim recently pointed out the implicit power of the chronological system in the English translation of Koselleck's essay "On the Need for Theory in the Discipline of History." The phrase "theory of historical times" (*geschichtlichen Zeiten*) becomes "theory of periodizations" (Jordheim 2012: 151–52). Periods, Newtonian duration, was the only theory of historical times imaginable.

17. Serres writes, "Two distant points suddenly are close, even superimposed. If, further, you tear it in certain places, two points that were close can become very distant" (Serres with Latour 1995: 60).

18. Several recent works on change, invention, and innovation argue that change often results from repetitive processes, collaboration, serendipity, and/or accidents (Ashton 2015; Kennedy 2016).

19. Sewell (2008) calls this bifurcated temporality "surprising" (520) or "weird" (533). It is only strange if one accepts chronological time of progress and newness.

20. Foley (2012) uses the metaphor of the agora, the ancient Greek notion of a site of exchange. He identifies three principal agoras: oral, textual, and electronic. The pathways project is accessible through its website, http://pathwaysproject.org. The same material is available in a book, *Oral Tradition and the Internet* (Foley 2012). The website is organized through networked associations; the book is organized alphabetically. Foley writes, "The common misconception that the advent of writing technology cues the immediate closure of the oAgora [oral exchange] has proven time and again to be nothing more than blind tAgora [textual exchange] bias. Writing is used initially for record-keeping and similar accounting procedures, most certainly not for preserving group and personal identity, remembering history, transmitting remedies for disease, and the myriad other social functions performed by oral traditions" (60).

21. I am thankful to Cornelius Holtorf for bringing this essay to my attention. My contact with Cornelius, ironically, was due in large part to the closed, rather than open, access to publications (and the affordances of the internet).

22. The early disdain for John Okada's powerful account of the dilemmas faced by Japanese Americans in the camps in *No-No Boy* ([1957] 1976) is indicative of this early attempt at forgetting.

23. For a fine example of multiple and layered times that come together a musical piece, see "The Nature of Time" by Lorren Stafford and Chris Strouth (2001).

24. By *science*, I am thinking of the human sciences.

CODA

1. Cornelia Vismann writes, "Those who work with records are familiar with the problem: files pile up on desks, accumulate in offices, and fill attics and basements. Though registered, their order collapses time and again; though collected, quashed, dispatched, sold, shredded, or destroyed in some other way, they keep mushrooming" (2008: xi).

2. There are many works that are troubled by social change and identify problems as the dysfunction wrought by technology (sometimes for good reason), such as Carr (2010), Turkle (2011), and Twenge (2017).

3. Henri Lefebvre writes that mobility and stability are contradictory but constituent elements of modernity (1995: 190).

4. An interesting problem in a major subfield of AI, deep learning, is the difficulty of algorithms making sense of "commonsense reasoning," while it excels in categorization (Marcus 2018). What if the categories are abstractions that organize life rather than those that have emerged from life?

5. Through my work in scholarly communications with the Force11 community, I cannot help but wonder whether the obsession with progress and innovation, fueled by digital technology, is akin to Lucy Ricardo and Ethel Mertz working on the candy production line in an episode of *I Love Lucy*: initially charmed by the ease of technology but increasingly pressured and ultimately frantic as production continues to accelerate.

6. See, for example, chapter 4 of Ethan Kleinberg's wonderfully titled book, *Haunting History*. He writes, "If anything, recent advances in the digital humanities have led us toward a resurgent neopositivism, chasing empiricist dreams toward the grail of history as a hard science" (2017: 118).

7. I riff this subheading from the title of Chris Lorenz's fine article on history and time that proposes we look for alternatives to "European chronocentrism" (2017). It is, of course, the title of a Bob Dylan song. I extend this search by considering how pasts are changing in the face of digital media.

8. For fine monographs on the relation of cybernetics and the humanistic sciences, see Hayles (1999) and Clarke (2009).

9. Jasanoff goes on to describe these technologies: "Humility instructs us to think harder about how to reframe problems so that their ethical dimensions are brought to light, which new facts to seek and when to resist asking science for clarification. Humility directs us to alleviate known causes of people's vulnerability to harm, to pay attention to the distribution of risks and benefits, and to reflect on the social factors that promote or discourage learning" (2007: 33).

Index

absolute time, 2–4, 6–7, 14, 16, 23–24, 26, 31–38, 40, 43, 49, 52, 54, 57, 59–64, 76, 86, 90, 96, 131, 177n1, 179n16, 183n41. *See also* classical time

acceleration, 129, 143, 153. *See also* compression of time and space

activity: and abstraction, 5, 7, 15, 18–20, 31–34, 38, 43, 47, 57, 65, 71, 80, 83, 88–89, 91, 95, 117, 133; documents as nodes of, 70, 75–76, 106; as condition of organisms and units, 119–120, 123, 125, 131, 141; as depicted in graphic novels, 108–109; and duration, 181n19; history as, 184n3; as unit of analysis, 100, 102, 104, 118–119, 124, 126, 131–132, 140–143. *See also* classical time; internal times

aggregates, 36, 40, 57, 138, 185n8

alibi, chronology as, 1, 2–3, 14, 90. *See also* occlusion; bewitching

allochronism, 31. *See also* classing

Anthropocene, 54, 96–98, 111, 132, 134, 184n1, 184n2, 189n17, 189n18, 191n14, 191n15

anticipation, 29, 53, 56, 154, 155

appropriation, 102–103, 106–107

archives, 14, 52, 63–64, 70, 72, 107, 127, 143, 149; digital, 7, 150, 153, 183n43; and the nation-state 74–75, 178n9, 186n28, 189n27

Aristotle, 33, 93

authority, 21, 32, 35, 61, 68

Bacon, Francis, 21, 22, 32, 35, 42, 60

before Christ (BC)/anno Domini (AD), 26, 92, 188n10

bells, 25, 34

Benjamin, Walter, 6, 14, 21, 24, 29, 51, 53, 59, 62–63, 73, 77, 81, 107–108, 109–110, 127, 154, 192n13, 183n43

Bergson, Henri, 41, 65–66, 95, 97, 114, 115, 116–117, 119, 122, 135, 145, 146, 182n34, 183n37, 190n2

Bertalanffy, Ludwig von, 45–46, 87, 94, 103, 105, 112, 124, 142, 144, 157, 158, 189n29, 191n8

bewitching, 53, 62, 65, 67. *See also* alibi, occlusion

dates, 11, 19, 53, 55, 71, 72, 73, 83, 92, 95, 102, 116, 133. *See also* homogenization; spatialization of time

de Cusa, Nicholas, 87, 112, 157, 190n36

decay, 19, 28, 44–45, 83, 118, 122, 123, 124, 134, 142, 145, 183

deep time, 11, 53, 112, 134, 156, 187n2, 189n18

Derrida, Jacques, 149, 155

development. *See* absolute time; classical time; classing of time and space

digital humanities, 6–7, 17, 18, 89, 102, 150, 177n5, 193n6

digital media, 7, 9, 10–11, 12, 18, 53, 87, 106, 110, 113, 136, 147, 149–151, 183n43, 193n7

Dionysus Exiguus, 26, 71, 180n10

distance. *See* classing; dates; documents; spatialization of time

documents, 10, 14, 17, 63–64, 70, 72–76, 92–93, 105–107, 152, 189n27. *See also* "facts"

duration, 29, 66, 83, 90, 94, 100, 119, 126, 141; Bergsonian, 95, 97, 117, 135, 182n34; Newtonian, 21, 32, 33, 40, 42, 65, 68, 94–96, 181n19, 192n16

East/West dichotomy, 37, 61, 137

Edo society, 26, 27

eigenzeit, 44, 94, 105. *See also* special relativity

Einstein, Albert, 23, 44, 94, 102–103, 105

Elias, Norbert, 2–3, 11, 18, 23, 35, 49, 90

emergence, 19, 93, 122, 125, 126, 140

empty time, 14, 63, 178n13

Enlightenment, the, 11, 15, 26–27, 37, 51, 53, 58, 62, 64, 75, 78, 87–88, 95, 110, 127, 138, 149, 151, 155, 156, 158

entropy, 19, 44–45, 120–125, 127, 134, 139, 183n43, 191n5, 191n6, 191n14

eternal present, 30

Eurocentrism, 59, 88, 95

evolution, 45, 48, 123–124, 126, 132, 138, 139, 183n43, 185n14

experience, elimination of by chronology, 10, 14, 32–33, 36, 48, 65, 79–80, 102, 107–108, 143–144; maintaining heterogeneity of, 11, 14, 58, 89, 91, 102, 107–109, 140, 142, 144, 186n19; and perception, 28, 29, 41–43, 75, 91, 98, 106, 109, 179n17; space of, 30, 93

externalization. *See* activity

"facts," 7, 9–10, 14, 20, 45, 62, 70–73, 75, 83, 98, 102, 118, 148, 152–154, 178n9; and situatedness, 105–106, 109, 125, 179n20, 186n23. *See also* documents; nation-state

France, 37, 68

Fraser, J. T., 1, 2, 5, 18–20, 33, 45, 79–80, 91, 94, 98, 105, 111, 145, 149, 179n2, 183n42, 187n7

Fukuzawa Yukichi, 135, 186n21

genealogy, 56, 184n4

general, the, 42, 61, 64, 74, 98, 108

General System Theory (GST), 45, 87, 123, 184n47

geographic space, 43, 51, 57, 58, 62, 65–66, 73, 108, 116. *See also* nation-state; spatialization of time

linear time. *See* absolute time; classical time; classing of time and space

location. *See* simple location; classing of time and space; spatialization of time

longue durée, 96–97, 100, 127, 188n16

machines, 34, 45–47, 104, 138, 154, 180n8, 187n1

Macy Conferences, 17, 45–46, 104–105, 123, 153–154, 183n38. *See also* cybernetics

mapping, 7, 41, 61, 73, 118. *See also* classing of space and time; nation-state; simple location

market, 38, 71, 101

Marx, Karl, 5, 67, 69, 81, 127, 130, 182n32, 186–187n18

mathematical time. *See* absolute time; classical time; spatialization of time

Mayan calendar, 27

meaning, 10, 12, 20, 25, 70–73, 75–76, 93, 99, 105–107, 136, 149, 151–154, 157, 178n9, 179n19. *See also* data; documents; information; Shannon, Claude; situatedness

measure. *See* absolute time; classical time; classification, chronology as technology of; classing of time and space; control

media archaeology, 9, 134, 134, 156

media inflation. *See* information

medieval times, 24–28, 56, 58, 101, 157; and complexity, 27, 44, 97; and privileging of the modern, 60–70, 95, 137. *See also* periodization

Meiji Japan, 27, 72, 109, 180, 182

memory, 11, 20, 29, 82, 99, 103, 147, 150

mobility, 30, 95, 117–119, 123, 125–127, 138, 141, 149, 193n3. *See also* duration; stability

modernity, 5, 23, 43, 59, 67, 80, 121, 143, 185n10, 185n12, 191n3, 193n3

Montesquieu, 57–58, 60, 185, 188

multiplicity, 2, 6, 8, 9, 14, 17–18, 40, 64, 85, 127, 140, 146, 151, 184n3. *See also* complexity; heterogeneity

Musil, Robert, 109, 142

mystics, 11, 32, 68, 81, 112–113, 151, 153, 156, 179n17

mythical mode of thought, history as, 3–5, 23, 76–77, 85, 109–111, 116, 120, 122, 127, 154–155, 158, 180n4

nation-state, 7, 9, 15–16, 23, 27, 37–39, 41–42, 44, 59, 62–63, 66–68, 73–74, 83, 85, 89, 93, 100, 117, 123, 131–133, 138, 144, 178n9, 183n39. *See also* archives; classing of time and space; spatialization of time; unit of analysis

naturalization of chronology. *See* absolute time; alibi; bewitching

new, the, 15, 42, 67, 69, 80–81, 87, 101, 112, 121, 126, 134, 150, 155, 185n10. *See also* innovation; old, the

Newton, Sir Isaac, 4, 21, 32, 35, 51, 56–59, 65, 116, 120, 156, 181n16, 184n7

Newtonian time. *See* absolute time; classical time; duration

nootemporality, 91, 105. *See also* *eigenzeit*

Nowotny, Helga, 43, 48, 72, 80, 87, 115, 119–120, 126, 136, 155, 179n2, 183n42, 185n10, 190n35 objectivity, 47, 61–62, 77, 102–103, 111–112, 152, 158. *See also* data; information; relationality

observer, 32–33, 44, 47, 76, 90–91, 94, 99, 102, 104–105, 111, 113, 125, 156–157, 189n28. *See also* cybernetics; perspectives; special relativity

occlusion. *See* alibi; bewitching

O'Donnell's Law, 7

old, the, 15, 61, 69, 86, 87, 112, 156, 185n10

Olympics, 26, 38, 71, 188n11

oral traditions, 29, 110, 192n20

order. *See* classification; classing of time and space

organic processes, 34–35, 36, 39, 88, 91, 123, 139–141, 143, 149

Orient and Occident, 37, 59–61, 68, 69, 132, 137, 157

originary state, 15, 31, 39, 56, 59, 73, 122, 141, 149

particular, the, 14, 49, 52, 61, 63–67, 73–74, 95

periodization, 54, 65, 94–96. *See also* classing of time and space; spatialization of time

perspectives, 9, 18, 44, 76, 87, 90, 100, 108, 114, 120, 132–133, 146, 149, 152–153, 156. *See also* activity; experience; meaning; observer; special relativity

Petavius, Domenicus, 26–27, 71, 72

philosophy of history, 59, 63–65, 89

political time, 23, 48, 62, 74, 77, 148, 188n16

prediction, 154–155. *See also* anticipation

presentism, 11, 47, 53, 80, 112, 136, 153. *See also* acceleration; compression of time and space

prime meridian, 36. *See also* International Meridian Conference (1884)

probability, 10, 36, 40, 138

progress. *See* absolute time; classical time; classing of time and space; innovation

qualitative mode of analysis, 10, 74, 95, 118, 126, 185n12. *See also* activity; Bergson, Henri; unit of analysis

qualities, 56, 93, 109, 113, 126, 133, 142; and boredom, 143

quantitative mode of analysis, 10, 17, 32, 38, 74, 95, 116. *See also* duration; spatialization of time and space

quantum physics, 4, 23–24, 44, 86, 112, 183n36, 187–188n7

railroad time, 37, 178

Ranke, Leopold von, 60–64, 72, 74–75, 77, 102, 143, 153. *See also* archives; documents

Rashomon, 106–107

reading, 4, 45, 99, 103–104, 111, 113, 151, 186n29

reality, 9, 11, 22, 23, 54–55, 60, 62, 65–66, 70, 73, 75, 79, 87, 105, 115–116, 119, 122, 145–146, 152. *See also* archives; change; experience; multiplicity

recording. *See* archives; documents; facts

relationality, 5, 19, 42, 44, 91, 106, 111, 129, 133, 146, 149, 151; elision of, 48, 61, 77

religion, 26, 180n8

repetition, 16–17, 19, 29, 31, 34, 35, 39–40, 45, 49, 56, 59, 66, 69–70, 82–83, 100–101, 122, 123–126, 132, 135, 140–143, 145, 150, 153, 155, 185n13. *See also* change; clock time; innovation; spatialization of time; stability

research, 70, 74, 128; historicization of, 19, 81–82, 95, 120, 179n17; obscuration of, 13–15, 52

rhythm, 5, 12, 18, 23, 24, 91, 94, 108, 137, 139, 178n6, 182n31

Rhythmanalysis. See rhythm

Roman world, 26, 59

Saint Simon, 59

scales, 66, 95–97, 99, 121, 124, 126, 129–133, 134, 144, 145, 191n12; of development, 39

Scaliger, Joseph, 26

scientific history, 60. *See also* archives; documents; facts; Ranke, Leopold von

second law of thermodynamics, 44, 120, 122. *See also* entropy

sequence, 3, 27, 51, 57, 65–66, 103, 116. *See also* boundary work; classing of time and space; linear time; spatialization of time

Serres, Michel, 2–4, 11, 16–18, 37–38, 40, 42, 59, 67–68, 77, 112, 114, 129, 133, 138–140, 144, 182n29, 185n18, 192n17. *See also* classing of time and space; turbulence

Shannon, Claude, 10, 20, 125, 152, 178n9

simple location, 41, 44, 46, 61–62, 64, 73, 98, 107, 127. *See also* classing of time and space

situatedness, 18, 19, 73, 76, 87, 91, 93, 98, 102, 103–105, 119, 140, 146, 151–153, 178n7. *See also* relationality

social time, 25, 26, 99

spatialization of time, 29, 39–40, 54–55, 57, 65–66, 94–95, 117–118, 128, 133–134, 138–139, 141, 145, 181n19, 188n15, 190n2. *See also* nation-state; stability

special relativity, 4, 23, 44, 86, 102–103

stability, 16–17, 29–30, 33, 39, 57, 70, 100, 112, 117, 123–124, 136, 138, 143, 149, 152, 193n3. *See also* repetition

standardization of time, 37, 75, 100

states, ontological in contrast to qualities, 93, 115, 116, 118, 124, 126, 132, 151

stories, 6, 14, 29, 73, 74, 82, 102, 107–110, 131, 132, 138

Strasbourg cathedral clock, 25

subsumption, 2, 36, 40, 54, 67, 69, 133, 145, 150, 184n2, 186n18

synchronization, 37, 91, 119, 128, 182n28, 188n11

tattered times, 126, 129, 139–140

taxonomy, 1, 3, 66, 148, 190n1

technology, 9, 10, 18, 40, 46, 48, 52, 95, 97, 101, 134–136, 148, 150, 155, 181n18, 185n14, 190n34, 190n20, 193n2, 193n5; chronology and history as, 5, 42–43, 55, 62, 77, 81, 90, 117

teleology, 13, 123

time-compact order, 79, 111, 145, 149

trade, 28, 31, 138

tradition, 2, 12, 15, 68, 103–104, 110, 149, 155, 192n20

translation, 27, 71, 92

tulip bubble of 1635–36, 135

turbulence, 129–130, 133, 140, 145

uncertainty, 9, 111, 157

unevenness of and in time, 14, 24–26, 37, 64, 77, 83, 86, 132, 187n1

unit of analysis, 44, 89, 90, 130; the nation-state as, 83. *See also* activity; nation-state

unitization of time. *See* classing of time and space

value system, 17, 48, 65, 73, 77, 91

violence, 38, 48, 54, 56, 57, 62, 70, 92, 109, 145

Voltaire, 59, 60, 63

von Foerster, Heinz, 46, 47, 104, 111, 113, 126, 129, 140

waste, 44, 121, 134, 183n43

White, Richard, 82–83, 95, 135

Whitehead, Alfred North, 41, 42, 44, 61, 62, 75, 79, 80, 92, 98, 128, 181n26, 182n33, 183n36

work, in industrial societies, 30, 34–35, 43, 101, 121, 143

Yasutsugu Shigeno, 72

CPSIA information can be obtained
at www.ICGtesting.com
Printed in the USA
FSHW011341200719
60230FS